MY ANCESTORS MOVED IN ENGLAND OR WALES:

HOW CAN I TRACE WHERE THEY CAME FROM?

Anthony J. Camp

Society of Genealogists

1994

Society of Genealogists

14 Charterhouse Buildings
Goswell Road
London EC1M 7BA

First published as
My ancestor was a migrant, 1987

Second revised edition, 1994

ISBN 0 946789 80 0

Acknowledgements: The first edition of this booklet benefited from comments made on an earlier draft by Christopher Watts. This edition has benefited from the suggestions of Elizabeth Silverthorne, Ruth Killon and Brian Christmas. For them the author is very grateful.

CONTENTS

A. FIRST CONSIDERATIONS

A.1. Introduction

Perhaps the genealogist's most difficult problem prior to 1851 is to trace the place of birth of an ancestor who appears at a certain place without giving any indication as to whence he came. The problem is much the same whether the ancestor moved from one neighbouring parish to another, from the country to the town, from Scotland to England, from England to Ireland, or from England to one of the colonies. The move is rarely recorded as such; the ancestor's place of origin has to be traced in other ways.

After 1851 a movement within England and Wales or in Scotland, and to some extent between them, may generally be traced by means of the census returns, but this is not the case in Ireland where the majority of returns prior to 1901 have not survived. This booklet attempts to set out the major record sources which may be used prior to 1851 to trace a movement within England and Wales. It assumes that the resources of the General Register Office after 1 July, 1837, have been exhausted. The death of any migrant ancestor who is likely to have survived to that date must be searched for there and the age at death, and thus the approximate date of birth, determined. The possibility of survival until one of the censuses was taken must always be considered. If the migrant lived through several censuses then all should be consulted, not only for differing statements as to place of birth but for the other reasons mentioned in **Section B.2.** below.

Available transcripts and indexes of the various census returns 1841-91 are listed in *Marriage, census and other indexes for family historians,* by J. Gibson and E. Hampson (FFHS, 4th edn. 1992). A project to transcribe, index and publish on microfiche the whole of the 1881 census returns for England, Wales and Scotland is making rapid progress.

Censuses and other lists of inhabitants in particular places compiled for various reasons unconnected with the national civil censuses of 1841-91 are listed in *Local census listings 1522-1930: holdings in the British Isles,* by J. Gibson and M. Medlycott (FFHS, 1992). Some provide ages, others may indicate relationships and very occasionally they include place of birth.

A.2. Married or Single?

The most important thing to consider is whether the person who moved went as a single man or whether he was married. If you have the marriage of two persons to look for you are a great deal more fortunate than if you are searching for the single entry of a baptism with all the problem of correct identification and proof which may be necessary once a possible candidate has been found.

The young man who moves prior to his marriage is perhaps the most difficult of all migrants to trace and identify with certainty. Indications of the places of origin of single people may, however, be found in many aspects of their later lives discussed in this booklet. These indications may appear at any time from education to death and may even be found in the next generation and beyond in the activities and connections of the children and grandchildren. All will need to be carefully considered. In addition movement is frequently found to be circulatory, the migrant returning to a former place of residence or to its neighbourhood.

A.3. International Genealogical Index: Baptisms

The only major centralised index of births or baptisms prior to 1 July, 1837, except those of nonconformists mentioned below (**Sections L.1., L.2., L.3.** and **L.5.**) and of the limited numbers recorded in some journals and newspapers (**Section B.6.**), is that mainly taken from parish registers and bishops transcripts but containing some privately submitted matter (not always reliable), compiled by the Genealogical Society of Utah and known as the International Genealogical Index (I.G.I.). A first edition was published on microfiche in 1976 and became widely available. Subsequent editions on microfiche and CD-ROM, the most recent in 1993, contain many millions of entries.

The Index has become the first place in which to search for the baptism of any person prior to 1837, and, as it continues to 1875, it often contains baptisms of persons in the early years of civil registration whose births were not registered or which escaped the manuscript indexes at the General Register Office. The full entry in the original source must always be consulted for possible additional information.

The Index does not normally extend beyond the period 1538-1875, there being, in the microfiche editions, one alphabetical sequence by surname and christian name for each county for the whole period. The variants of surnames are generally brought together but great care should be taken to see that all the possible variants have been checked. Abbreviated and Latin forms of christian names appear and are easily overlooked in the general alphabetical sequence. The CD-ROM editions index the British Isles in one alphabetical sequence regardless of county but may select slightly different groupings of surname variants from those on the microfiche. The parish coverage of the Index, which varies considerably from county to county and is not complete for any county, can be ascertained from *Parish and vital records listings,* published on microfiche.

The 1992 edition of the Index is widely available on microfiche at county record offices and libraries. The larger 1993 edition on CD-ROM may be found at many branch Family History Centres of the Genealogical Society of Utah.

A.4. Boyd's Marriage Index

If the migrant moved after his marriage then the first place to start looking for that marriage is probably the typescript Marriage Index compiled by Percival Boyd at the Society of Genealogists. It has about seven million entries: possibly twelve per cent of all the marriages in England in the period 1538-1837. The Index has a more than fifty per cent coverage in the counties of Cambridgeshire, Cornwall, Durham, Essex, Gloucestershire, Isle of Wight, Middlesex and London, Northumberland, Oxfordshire, Shropshire and Suffolk, but often only before 1812 or 1754. It includes some marriages from every county, but has a less than ten per cent coverage in Bedfordshire, Berkshire, Herefordshire and Staffordshire. It covers no part of Scotland, Wales or Ireland.

The Index is divided into ten periods, then by county, and then by surname, the marriage entries then being in chronological order. The entries are usually indexed both by the men and the women, sometimes in separate volumes. Entries not found in this First [County] Series may be found in two additional Miscellaneous Series, subdivided in the same manner. Care must be exercised to make sure that all the relevant periods and spellings have been checked, variants generally being brought together under phonetic spellings.

So far as they are known the parishes and periods covered by the Index are shown in *A list of parishes in Boyd's marriage index* (Society of Genealogists, 6th edn. 1987). The earlier editions of this list should not be used. It contains details of the other marriage indexes added to the main series at the Society of Genealogists since Mr. Boyd's death (excepting only the complete index for Oxfordshire 1538-1837 received in 1987) and shows where some county copies of the main series may be found. There is a complete typescript copy of the Index in the Library of the Genealogical Society of Utah in Salt Lake City and microfiche copies are widely available in many Family History Centres and other libraries.

A.5. Local Marriage Indexes

A large number of marriage indexes for various parts of the British Isles have recently been compiled to supplement Boyd's work. Most are in private hands or in those of local family history societies, and a few are complete (e.g. Isle of Wight, Hertfordshire, Oxfordshire, Staffordshire), while others are complete for certain periods only (e.g. Kent). The Pallot Marriage Index, almost complete for the London area, 1780-1837, is in the possession of the Institute of Heraldic and Genealogical Studies. Few of these indexes go beyond 1837 (when the centralised civil registration of marriages commenced at the General Register Office) though a notable exception is the index of Roman Catholic marriages in London and Essex 1837-75 at the Institute of Heraldic and Genealogical Studies. Details of these indexes and the conditions under which they may be consulted are given in *Marriage, census and other indexes for family historians,* by J. Gibson (FFHS, 4th edn. 1992).

A.6. International Genealogical Index: Marriages

A large number of marriage entries, taken mainly from parish registers and bishops transcripts, appears on recent editions of the International Genealogical Index (*see above* **Section A.3**). Although the Index contains many more baptisms than marriages there are many millions of entries and it should be used in conjunction with Boyd's Marriage Index and any local marriage index. The most recent, 1993 edition, should be used.

A.7. Marriage Licences

Failing the above indexes the marriage licences which have not been included in them should be searched. Licences were issued by archbishops, bishops, archdeacons and other ecclesiastics and the centralised records and calendars which they compiled often form marriage indexes for very large areas. The whereabouts of these, together with details of those published, transcribed and microfilmed, is given in *Bishops transcripts and marriage licences: bonds and allegations: a guide to their location and indexes,* by J.S.W. Gibson (FFHS, 3rd edn. 1991).

The local marriage licences issued by the archdeacons (some did not have the power to issue licences) and bishops should be consulted first, and then those issued by the Vicar Generals of the two Provinces of Canterbury and York (for parties who came from differing dioceses in the same Province) and by the Faculty

Office of the Archbishop of Canterbury (for parties who came from differing Provinces).

The licences issued by the Vicar General of the Archbishop of Canterbury are at Lambeth Palace Library, London, and commence in 1660. They have been published to 1694, and are included in Boyd's Marriage Index to 1709. The records have been published on microfiche and there are microfilms of the calendars only 1709-1839 at the Society of Genealogists.

The licences issued by the Vicar General of the Archbishop of York are at the Borthwick Institute of Historical Research, York, and commence in 1660. They are not covered by Boyd's Marriage Index, though William Paver's nineteenth-century extracts of marriage licences which have since disappeared (1567-1714) are covered by Boyd's Index. Valuable abstracts of the Archbishop of York's licences have been published 1765-1839 as *An index to the Archbishop of York's marriage bonds and allegations,* by E.B. and W.R. Newsome (4 vols. 1986-89) and E.B. Newsome (3 vols. 1990-93).

The licences issued by the Faculty Office are at Lambeth Palace Library and are fragmentary before 1632. They have been published from 1534 to 1714 and are included in Boyd's Marriage Index from 1543 to 1714. The records have been published on microfiche and there are microfilms of the calendars only 1714-1845 at the Society of Genealogists.

The printed, manuscript and microfilm indexes in the possession of the Society of Genealogists are listed in *Marriage licences: abstracts and indexes in the library of the Society of Genealogists,* by L. Collins (Society of Genealogists, 4th edn. 1991).

Between 1754 and 1837 every marriage, to be a legal marriage, excepting only those of Quakers and Jews, had to take place in the parish church according to the rites of the Church of England, and so any nonconformist (Baptist, Presbyterian, Wesleyan, even a Roman Catholic) wishing some privacy and to avoid the indignity of having banns called on three successive Sundays, is more likely to have married by licence than by banns, an important point when searching for the marriage of any nonconformist. Licences were commonly used by couples in a hurry to marry, those wishing to marry away from their usual places of residence, those marrying spouses of differing age, religion or social standing, and those wishing to marry in Lent.

For a short period from 15 September 1822 to 26 March 1823 (when bonds for marriage licences were abolished) baptismal certificates were required when marriage licences were applied for. Very occasionally in the same short period the affidavits of those requesting banns to be published (to be found, if they have survived, with the parish records) give additional information to the banns and marriage entries.

A.8. Proximity of London

The anonymity which London provided has always been a great draw for anyone needing to marry in privacy and when a particular marriage cannot be found, especially in the south-east of England, then the possibility of marriage in London should be considered and the appropriate indexes and registers checked. Such a marriage would not necessarily have been by licence.

Prior to 1754 marriage in London without formality of banns or licence was available at a small number of centres, including the Fleet Prison. More than half the marriages which took place in the metropolis were celebrated at these centres. See *Irregular marriage in London before 1754,* by T. Benton (Society of Genealogists, 1993). Many of these marriages relate to people from the London suburbs and from surrounding counties.

A.9. General Comment

It should be remembered that the transcribers of marriage registers do not always search the banns registers. The banns entries for those marriages which did not take place in the parish will therefore have been omitted. These banns entries will, however, lead to the marriage entries in the other parties' parishes. After 1754, from which date separate banns registers are likely to have survived, this point should be taken into consideration when the location of any marriage is being sought.

Once the marriage itself has been found, or if the first entry you have on your pedigree is a marriage, then you must ask yourself if that marriage was by banns or by licence, and look at the banns book or at the licence, the bond and the allegation. Note also, of course, the witnesses which will appear in any marriage entry in parish registers after 1754. Any one of these sources may hold some additional clue. Marriages by licence, such additional information, and entries of banns for which no marriage took place, it must be noted, are not necessarily copied into the bishops transcripts of parish registers.

A.10. Divorce

If a couple were divorced the record of the proceedings would normally say where and when their marriage had taken place. Prior to 1858 a consistory court might grant a legal separation on grounds of life- threatening cruelty or adultery by the husband or of adultery by the wife, when alimony might be enforced through the Court of Chancery. This would not allow re-marriage. However, a marriage might be dissolved (allowing re-marriage) if not consummated within two years or for impotence or frigidity or if it could be shown to be incestuous or bigamous, again in the consistory court.

Many such cases were heard by the Court of Arches and there is a printed calendar in J. Houston, *Index of cases in the records of the Court of Arches at Lambeth Palace Library 1660-1913* in Index Library, vol. 85 (British Record Society, 1972). An appeal might also go to the Court of Delegates before 1832 and between 1833 and 1858 to the Judicial Committee of the Privy Council in which case the records are at the Public Record Office, Chancery Lane.

Since the late seventeenth century it has been possible to obtain a divorce allowing re-marriage by Act of Parliament but this entailed considerable expense as from the 1780s it normally (and from 1798 always) followed actions for criminal conversation in a civil court as well as for adultery in the ecclesiastical court. Those in the period 1801-1947 are indexed in *Index to local and personal Acts* (London, 1949), pp.1065- 68.

Civil divorce, allowing re-marriage, was made possible in 1858 and the files 1858-1937 with indexes 1858-1958 are at the Public Record Office, Chancery Lane. The former are open to search after 75 years.

In the eighteenth century a private deed of separation might be used by persons of property which effectively allowed re-marriage or cohabitation without fear of prosecution, but very few such records survive. Artisans in the eighteenth century and poor labourers in the early nineteenth century might resort to divorce by mutual consent in the public selling of their wives but the procedure was sufficiently rare to be reported in newspapers.

Divorces reported in *The Times* are indexed in *Index to Divorces (as listed in Palmer's Index to "The Times"): 1788-1910,* by About Archives (Leeming, Western Australia, 1989).

B. LATER LIFE

The later history of the migrant must next be considered. People did not normally go through their adult lives and die without some contact with their brothers and sisters, uncles, aunts and cousins. Even the children of a migrant will probably maintain some connections with the areas from which their fathers came or return there. Often a migrant's child visiting his uncles or aunts or cousins will marry someone from their areas and thus give a clue to the family's general place of origin.

B.1. Children

The details of the children of the migrant must be searched out in detail, with their wives and other family connections. The entries of baptism of some younger children may provide greater detail about the parents than those of the older ones, and if they were born in Durham or Northumberland between 1798 and 1812, for instance, the fuller baptismal entries will show the places of birth of both parents. The same is true to a lesser extent following the introduction of William Dade's form of registration in 1777 in some parts of Yorkshire and Nottinghamshire. Such extra detail may not be copied into bishops transcripts, so beware if your searches are being done through that source (or the International Genealogical Index) alone.

Nonconformist registers of birth and baptism vary considerably from entry to entry in the details they give of parentage or origin and should always be searched over a wide period.

B.2. Parents

In the same manner, parents do not easily lose touch with their children. They may need their support in later life. From 1834 onwards, the children may be ordered to give that support by the Guardians of the Poor Law Union in which they lived (*see below* **Section K.3.**), or the parents may go to live with their children. Thus you must search all the census returns available between 1841 and 1891, not just one of the returns to discover a particular place of birth, but every available return to see what members of the family or cousins have come into your ancestral household to be supported, perhaps, by the younger generation. A 'Visitor' or 'Boarder' in the census is often a relation in disguise. Not only that but a wider search in the census returns of the area into which a person comes to live may well reveal other relations already in the vicinity and a search of the whole enumeration district is frequently worthwhile.

B.3. Burials

Prior to 1851 you must also search the burial registers of the place in which your ancestor appears to see if his parents came also late in life to that parish and were buried there. Any stray entries of the same surname in the burial registers are always worth following up; the burials of children who were not baptised but whose baptisms might be found elsewhere, those of apparently unrelated persons from some named place, a stray spinster sister, anything of this nature may give a clue.

It seems a general fault in much genealogical research that the burial registers are not sufficiently widely searched for clues of this kind and that sufficient consideration is not given to other persons of the same surname found in the parish in which the migrant appears.

Several local family history societies and some individuals are now compiling burial indexes for particular areas or counties, usually prior to 1837. About a quarter of a million adult males in the London area are indexed in Boyd's London Burials 1538-1853, a typescript of which is at the Society of Genealogists, and this is supplemented by C.R. Webb's microfiche *City of London Burials 1813-53* (West Surrey Family History Society, 1991) which covers 75 of the 98 parishes. Such indexes are listed in *Marriage, census and other indexes for family historians,* by J. Gibson (FFHS, 4th edn. 1992).

B.4. Wills

At the end of the migrant's life his will, if he left one, may well mention land or relatives in some other part of the country, or the marriage contract of himself or his parents, or the latters' graves, or perhaps even make a bequest to the poor of the place where he was born. In earlier times any bequest of money to another parish, to the poor, to the bellringers, or to the church, would almost certainly indicate some close family connection with that place.

The mention of land in another parish should always be investigated for it may have been purchased or leased prior to migration or, more importantly, inherited from some previously unknown relative or ancestor. The exact relationship of any 'kinsman' mentioned in the will must also be investigated as also witnesses with the same surname who are not mentioned in the will. If a testator moves after making a will this is recorded in the Probate Act Book.

If a man leaves a will it is more than likely that his surviving widow will follow his example, and her will, or the will of a child of the migrant, may give clues similar to those mentioned above. The will of a married woman made in the lifetime of her husband will generally give the date of her marriage contract and some indication, in its recitation of the names of the parties to that contract, of her maiden name. The wills of unmarried women are frequently very informative about family relationships and possessions and should not be neglected.

With the creation of the Legacy or Estate Duty Office in 1796 and the levying of duties which varied according to the relationship of the recipient to the deceased the extracts of wills and administrations which were then created (the 'Death Duty Registers') were annotated with details of relationships which may not be given in the wills themselves. Not all the records prior to 1812 have survived but from that date there are consolidated national indexes and from 1815 they include practically all wills and administrations. The records, 1796-1903, are at the Public Record Office, Chancery Lane, and are described in Jane Cox, *Wills, inventories and death duties: the records of the Prerogative Court of Canterbury and the Estate Duty Office: a provisional guide* (PRO, 1988) and in Public Record Office Records Information Leaflet Number 66 (1987).

A person who went abroad or to Ireland or Scotland or even who died at sea and left property still in England may mention it directly in his will showing exactly where he came from, or there may be a second grant of probate of that will in the English courts. That is most likely to be in the Prerogative Court of Canterbury though it might be in the Prerogative Court of York if the migrant came from the Northern Province or in the local consistory court of his home area (particularly if that were London).

The same applies to those who went in the last century to Australia, New Zealand, Canada or South Africa, and to those who were killed abroad, in the South African and other wars. If they left property here or had a month's pay due their wills or administrations would (after January 1858) be in the Principal Probate Registry at Somerset House, as the printed indexes there frequently testify, showing the whereabouts of related beneficiaries and administrators in this country.

If the migrant had money in the public funds between 1717 and 1845 his will may be found in the Bank of England Will Extracts now at the Society of Genealogists. See *An index to the Bank of England will extracts 1807-45* (Society of Genealogists, 1991). An index for the earlier period is in preparation.

There are indexes to most wills prior to 1858 at the Society of Genealogists. For the whereabouts of original wills and a guide to published indexes see *Wills and their whereabouts,* by A.J. Camp (London, 1974) and *A simplified guide to probate jurisdictions: where to look for wills,* by J.S.W. Gibson (FFHS, 3rd edn. 1989).

B.5. Monumental Inscriptions

If there is no will, perhaps there is a monumental inscription or tombstone showing the deceased's place of origin, something more popular on the graves of those who have moved long distances than on the graves of those who stayed at home. An age or date of birth in an inscription, however, was not given by the person commemorated and should always be treated with caution.

Before going to the place of burial enquire as to copies of the inscriptions (which may have been made when they were more legible) at the county record office and local family history society. For the largest collection of copies of such inscriptions see *Monumental inscriptions in the library of the Society of Genealogists* (2 parts, Society of Genealogists, 1982 and 1987).

B.6. Newspaper Obituaries

In the last hundred years or so an obituary in a local newspaper may say something about the earlier life and place of origin of the deceased if he was of the shopkeeping or professional classes. For the whereabouts of copies of newspapers see *Local newspapers 1750-1920: a select location list,* by J.S.W. Gibson (FFHS, 1991) and the 'Gazetteer of English and Welsh newspapers 1690-1981' in *Town records,* by J. West (1983). The British Library's detailed *Bibliography of British newspapers* as yet only covers the counties of Derbyshire (1987), Durham and Northumberland (1982), Kent (1982), Nottinghamshire (1987) and Wiltshire (1982).

Occasionally earlier obituaries give such information and a useful partial index to many contemporary journals such as *The gentleman's magazine, The London magazine, The European magazine* and *The annual register* is the *Obituary prior to 1800,* compiled by Sir William Musgrave (Harleian Society, vols. 44-49, 1899-1901).

The Society of Genealogists has indexes of births, marriages and deaths reported in *The Times,* 1785-1933 (with the announcements themselves to 1920) on microfilm, with yearly manuscript indexes to the deaths 1894-1931.

C. TRAINING AND OCCUPATION

The occupation of the migrant person must next be considered. Did that occupation require some specialised training at school or university or by apprenticeship which might itself leave a record and show early origins or parentage, or was some licence required to practise it which might show movement from place to place?

C.1. Schools and Universities

The registers of most National Schools (from 1811) or local elementary schools (from 1870), where they have survived, will probably be too late to help us much. They may not show much more than age and, occasionally, place of previous education. School log books (from 1862) may survive in greater numbers but give less individual information. The registers of an earlier local grammar or charity school may survive and show age or date of birth, and perhaps father's name, place of residence and occupation. A few have been transcribed and published. Enquiries should be made at the county record office and at the school. The existence of such a school would be indicated in a local Kelly's or Post Office directory.

For the professional classes the same information will be given in the registers of a public (i.e. fee-paying) school, to which the student might travel many miles. Fortunately the registers of many have been published. Like university records they generally give the age of the student, his place of education, and his father's name, occupation and place of residence. The admission registers of the ancient British universities have been published, Oxford from earliest times to 1892, Cambridge to 1900, Trinity College, Dublin, 1593-1860, Aberdeen graduates 1495-1925, Glasgow matriculations 1728-1858 and graduates 1727-1897, Edinburgh graduates 1587-1888, and St Andrews graduates 1413-1579 and matriculations 1473-1579 and 1747-1897. The registers of the individual colleges within the universities rarely give additional information but again may have been published.

For a bibliography of published records see *Registers of the universities, colleges and schools of Great Britain and Ireland,* by P.M. Jacobs (London, Institute of Historical Research, 1964). The Society of Genealogists has one the largest collections of these records, listed in *School, university and college registers and histories in the library of the Society of Genealogists* (Society of Genealogists, 1988).

C.2. Apprentices

If the migrant was in a trade that needed a formal apprenticeship one is to some extent lucky, at least in the period 1710-1804. The stamp duty levied on the premiums paid between those dates resulted in a centralised record for the whole of the British Isles, now at the Public Record Office, Kew. The period 1710-74 has been transcribed and indexed by the Society of Genealogists and has been published on microfiche. The later period remains unindexed and may involve very lengthy searches. An index to the names of the masters for the period 1710-62, also at the Society, occasionally enables a master to be traced from one place to another if he took a series of apprentices in those years. An index for the period 1762-74 is nearing completion.

Unfortunately a premium was not paid when the apprentice was bound to his father or some other relative and stamp duty was not payable on the premiums of parish and charity apprentices. The ledgers recording the payment of the duty only show the parentage of the apprentice between 1710 and about 1752.

The indentures of pauper children placed as apprentices by the Overseers of the Poor in a parish prior to 1834 may remain with the parish records, some details may be given in the Accounts of the Overseers, or a separate register recording all the details may have been kept. Most would, however, have been destroyed at the completion of the usual seven-year apprenticeship. For the apprenticeship of pauper children sent from London to Lancashire, Cheshire, Nottinghamshire and Glasgow, *see* **Section K.3.** *below.*

Apprenticeship was and is basically a private contract. Outside the period 1710-1804, therefore, the great majority of apprentices, particularly in country areas, have gone unrecorded, though the indentures may survive by chance in the family or in the records of the employer. The Society of Genealogists has a miscellaneous collection of several thousand original indentures (mainly collected from parish records) in the period 1641-1888, and many others have found their way into county record offices.

C.3. Freemen

In cities and boroughs the corporation often controlled and enrolled apprenticeships which usually led to freedom of the borough. This gave one the right to trade in the borough and a vote at borough and Parliamentary elections. Freedom might usually be obtained by inheritance (patrimony), by apprenticeship to a freeman (servitude), or by purchase (redemption), and in some places by marriage to the widow or daughter of a freeman. For the first two categories the details enrolled usually give the father's name and place of residence and the records will be found amongst those of the town in question.

The towns involved are listed in *Town records,* by J. West (1983). Those published beyond 1660 include Canterbury (1392-1900), Chester (1392-1805), Exeter (1266-1967), Gloucester (1641-1838), Great Yarmouth (1429-1800), Guildford (1655-1933), King's Lynn (1292-1836), Lancaster (1688- 1840), Leicester (1196-1930), Newcastle-upon-Tyne (1409-1710), Norwich (1548-1752) and York (1272-1759). For a bibliography see *Freemen of England,* by H. Ward (1975).

A published Poll Book (*see below* **Section I.4.**) will give the names of those who, being free, voted at a Parliamentary election. It may have a separate section of non-resident freemen giving a valuable indication of movement away from the Town.

C.4. Gilds and Companies

In some cities and boroughs the gild or company records may also survive, giving similar details. Most companies had lost much of their importance by the eighteenth century if not by the seventeenth, and their records are rarely helpful in nineteenth-century genealogy. A few, however, retained a considerable measure of control and their records, as with the Cutlers Company in Sheffield, are particularly valuable, see *History of the Company of Cutlers in Hallamshire in the county of York,* by R.E. Leader (2 vols. 1906). There is a useful 'Gazetteer of sources on medieval gilds and trade 1066-1600' in *Town records,* by J. West.

C.5. The London Livery Companies

The records of the Livery Companies in London form one of the chief means by which persons coming into the City to practise a trade may be traced to their places of origin. The records of one or two, like the Society of Apothecaries (whose Licentiateship was a national qualification after 1815) and the Company of Watermen and Lightermen (which had a monopoly on the River Thames), even contain baptismal certificates of their apprentices. The records of the great majority of the London Companies are in the Guildhall Library and are described in their *Guide to the archives of the Livery Companies and related organisations in Guildhall Lbrary* (London, 2nd edn. 1983).

A centralised index to the London Company registers from 1681 to 1682, 1688 to October 1776, and from 1784 to the present day, showing those who proceeded to the Freedom of the City, is to be found in the Freedom Order Papers, Indentures, and Freedom Minute Books amongst the records of the Chamberlain's Court in the Corporation of London Records Office. These are particularly useful as one did not necessarily belong to the Company whose trade one practised. A printed Poll Book may here again be helpful, showing both the trade and the Company. See 'The City of London Freedom Registers', by M.T. Medlycott in *The genealogists' magazine,* vol. 19 (1977), pp. 45-7 and 141-2.

It should not be thought that these records are limited to professionals or craftsmen and that all lived in the City of London. They contain many small shopkeepers, street hawkers, mariners, and even some labourers. Many freemen lived in the East and West Ends of London and south of the Thames and, from the late eighteenth century, in the Home Counties and further afield. Unmarried women and widows often appear, particularly milliners with their own businesses and widows carrying on their husbands' trades.

In any case about two-thirds of the London City Companies had areas of authority outside the City, mostly varying from two to ten miles in radius, but sometimes much wider in extent. The Tylers and Bricklayers' Company had a fifteen-mile radius, the Fanmakers' twenty miles, the Horners' twenty-four miles, and the Gold and Silver Wyre Drawers' thirty miles. Four had an authority in the City of Westminster as well as in London. The Parish Clerks' covered London, Westminster, the Borough of Southwark and fifteen other parishes. The Watermen and Lightermen had authority over both banks of the Thames from Windsor to Gravesend; the Tacklehouse and Ticket Porters and the Fellowship Porters had authority in the Thames estuary up to the City. Members of the Vintners' Company could keep taverns in a number of cities and towns throughout England, and the Tobacco Pipe Makers' and Framework Knitters' had authority throughout England and Wales.

Some other London Companies had national roles and thus drew members from a wide area: the Goldsmiths' (and to a lesser extent the Needlemakers', Pewterers' and Pinmakers'), the Stationers', the Gunmakers', the Barber Surgeons' (entrusted from 1606 to 1745 with examining surgeons in the Royal Navy) and, as mentioned above, the Apothecaries' after 1815.

See the general guide mentioned above and *The gilds and companies of London,* by G. Unwin (1908, reprinted 1966), *The Livery Companies of the City of London,* by W.C. Hazlitt (1892) and 'The archives of the City of London Livery Companies and related organisations', by C.R.H. Cooper in *Archives,* vol.16 (1984), pp. 323-53.

C.6. Trade Unions

As previously mentioned apprenticeship records are of little assistance in the nineteenth century, the great majority not having survived. Towards the end of the century some trade union records (which normally only show age, occupation and the name of the employing company) begin to show movement of working men from place to place (in the transference of membership from one union branch to another) and some migration abroad (where the union had branches overseas) but these survive only sporadically.

The records of the craft unions may give more detail and may survive from an earlier date, but none are found before the 1830s following the repeal of the Combination Acts in 1825.

For example, the printed *Registration of members* (Typographical Association, Manchester, 1911) shows where their apprenticeships were served, their dates of joining the Association (some dating from 1865) with their ages at that time, as well as the branches where they were admitted and their branches in 1911.

Union branch records may be held or deposited locally, but many national records are deposited at the Modern Records Centre, University of Warwick Library, Coventry CV4 7AL. See *Trade union and related records: University of Warwick,* by J. Bennett and R. Storey (6th edn. 1991).

C.7. Directories

From about 1770 the movements of master craftsmen and tradesmen within a particular city and from about 1820 within a county may be traced from their inclusion in trade directories. As the nineteenth century proceeds many include consolidated lists by county. From the 1840s onwards this should at least enable one to find a person's place of birth from the appropriate census return.

For the years and areas for which directories survive and the whereabouts of copies see *Guide to the national and provincial directories of England and Wales excluding London, published before 1856,* by J.E. Norton (Royal Historical Society, 1950), *British directories 1850-1950,* by G. Shaw and A. Tipper

(University of Exeter, 1989) and *The London directories 1677-1855*, by C.W.F. Goss (London, 1932). See also the *Catalogue of directories and poll books in the possession of the Society of Genealogists* (Society of Genealogists, 1989).

C.8. Advertisements

The regular advertisements in a newspaper of a tradesman and others, from the proprietors of circulating libraries to dancing masters, may inadvertently show their movements from one place to another. Innkeepers and publicans may advertise an intended move hoping to take trade with them. Details of the whereabouts of runs of newspapers and of the few indexes to them yet available will be found in the works mentioned above in **Section B.6. Newspaper Obituaries.**

D. THOSE NEEDING A LICENCE FROM QUARTER SESSIONS

A publican who advertises an intended move may perhaps equally be traced (if he remains in the same county) through the licences issued by a magistrate at Quarter Sessions and there are various other categories of person who needed a yearly licence in order to practise their trade. The licence itself will not show parentage or movement from place to place but a regular run of licences issued to a person in one place followed immediately by another to a person of the same name in another place is very strong circumstantial evidence of movement.

The whereabouts of these groups of records may be determined from *Quarter sessions records for family historians: a select list,* by J.S.W. Gibson (FFHS, 3rd edn. 1992). Their historical background is described in *Guide to the Hertfordshire Record Office: part 1: quarter sessions and other records in the custody of the officials of the county,* edited by W. Le Hardy (Hertford, 1961).

D.1. Publicans

From 1552 Justices of the Peace were authorised to select the persons who should be given the right to keep a common alehouse and to take up with them a bond of surety or recognizance for the proper and orderly keeping of such houses. Licences were granted at Petty Sessions and the records may not be very complete even after the Statute of 1753 which required the Clerk of the Peace to keep a register of the recognizances filed. This would normally give the name of the landlord and, in some areas, the inn sign.

The restrictions on opening alehouses were removed in 1830 and the powers of the Justices to control them become largely inoperative until 1869 (though a modest control of Beer Shops was reimposed in 1840). Since 1869 there has been a much stricter control of all licensed premises. This control remained with the Quarter Sessions even after the establishment of County Councils in 1888.

D.2. Music and Dancing

Establishments for music and dancing have been similarly licensed since 1752.

D.3. Badgers, Higglers, Drovers, Hawkers, Pedlars

Dealers in corn and other commodities were also required to have licences under an Act of 1562, and to provide bonds and sureties for their behaviour. The Clerk of the Peace was required to keep a register book for presentation at Quarter Sessions showing the fees taken and the number of licences granted, and so a better record of them is often found. Those licensed were called badgers (dealers in corn or victuals), higglers or kidders (hawkers of corn and dead victuals) and drovers (drivers of cattle; supposed to be married men and householders). Their registration ended in 1772.

Hawkers had to have annual Revenue licences from 1698 but no regular record of those payments seems to have survived. Pedlars had to have annual police certificates from 1871 and hawkers (who were then differentiated as travelling with a horse) from 1888. From these dates details may be found with police records in county record offices.

D.4. Shopkeepers

In some areas the names of small shopkeepers may be found in the later records (prior to 1772) with those of the itinerant dealers. Slaughter houses were licensed by Quarter Sessions from 1786 and in the course of the nineteenth century several other categories came under regulation and had to have licences (not always from the local authority) though the records may not always survive. Those who sold game were licensed from 1831, those who sold explosives and fireworks from 1860 and petroleum from 1862 (local authority licences from 1871) and the proprietors of bakehouses from 1863. Other records may arise with the growth of local authority involvement in the control of the sale of perishable goods, the adulteration of food (from 1860), etc.

D.5. Barge and Wherry Owners

Barge and wherry owners, on navigable rivers and canals, were also registered by Quarter Sessions from 1795 to 1871, though the boats had to be above thirteen tons.

D.6. Printers

Under an Act of 1799 for the more effectual suppression of societies established for seditious and treasonable purposes printers were required to send to the Clerk of the Peace a declaration of the existence of their presses or their intention to set up a press. The system continued to 1869 and the records show the names and abodes of their owners, being brief records of the publishers of local newspapers and such like.

D.7. Freemasons

The same Act in 1799 required the names of Freemasons to be sent annually to Quarter Sessions, but the membership lists and registers of the Lodges at this early date are usually very incomplete. Such lists continue amongst Sessions records in some counties until at least the end of the last century. They are not indexed by county and are unlikely to provide evidence of movement.

The records of the Lodges themselves, however, if they can be located and access gained, may show movement from one Lodge to another both inside and out of the British Isles. It may be possible for the Secretary, The United Grand Lodge of England, Freemasons Hall, Great Queen Street, London, W.C.2, to confirm membership of a particular Lodge.

D.8. Gamekeepers

By the provisions of an Act of 1710 for the better preservation of Game the lord or lady of a manor could appoint one gamekeeper with power or authority to kill or destroy the game thereof, and the name of the gamekeeper had to be registered with the Clerk of the Peace. The Act has not been repealed but seems not to have been observed after about 1860, though later entries are occasionally found.

D.9. Gun Licences

A landowner who wished to carry a gun could do so if he had the right property qualification: a 40s. freehold from 1389, a £100 freehold or £150 long leasehold from 1670 to 1831. From 1831 anyone who paid for a game certificate was entitled to kill game subject to the law of trespass. Again the licence was granted at Quarter Sessions and a succession of licences may show movement from place to place but these people are likely to be more easily traced in other records.

D.10. Brokers

In London the Court of Aldermen of the City had the right (by Statutes of 1697, 1707 and 1817, restricted in 1870 and abolished in 1884) to license brokers of all kinds, including stockbrokers, ship and insurance brokers, cotton, tea, sugar and wool brokers, but not pawnbrokers. There are Admissions 1708-1869 showing addresses, and bonds 1697-1870, with other records, at the Corporation of London Records Office.

D.11. Pawnbrokers

Although pawnbrokers had to have annual Revenue licences from 1786, records seem only to survive after the Pawnbrokers' Act in 1872 which required a magistrate's certificate of good character. Such records may sometimes then be found in county record offices.

D.12. Chimney Sweeps

Chimney sweeps were required from 1875 to have annual police certificates and details may then be found with police records in county record offices.

E. THOSE NEEDING A LICENCE FROM A BISHOP

In the way that licences given by Quarter Sessions may show movement within a county, the Subscription Books of Bishops may, often in rather a fragmentary way, show the licensing and movements of others within a diocese.

E.1. Schoolmasters, Physicians, Surgeons, Midwives, Parish Clerks

Canons of 1604 codified earlier Acts which required the clergy and others to subscribe to the Thirty Nine Articles of religion and from that date if not earlier many schoolmasters and the occasional physician, surgeon and midwife as well as parish clerks and sextons are to be found in diocesan 'Subscription Books'. The main Act of 1511 was not repealed until 1948, but its provisions had fallen into gradual disuse. Physicians, surgeons and midwives do not normally appear after about 1750, schoolmasters continue to about 1850, and parish clerks to about the end of the century. The books themselves will be found with the other diocesan records, usually in county record offices. The information about schoolmasters may be supplemented from the Bishops' Visitation records, at least prior to the Restoration in 1660. For examples see *Norwich subscription books,* by E.H. Carter (1937), *Medical practitioners in the diocese of London ... 1529-1725,* by J.H. Bloom and P.R. James (1935), *Canterbury licences (general) 1568-1646,* by A.J. Willis (1972) and 'A register of schools and schoolmasters in the county of Cambridge, 1574-1700', by Elizabeth Key in the *Proceedings of the Cambridge Antiquarian Society* (1981).

F. LOCAL AND CENTRAL GOVERNMENT EMPLOYEES

F.1. Petitions

Some who had to subscribe to the Thirty Nine Articles would already have submitted a petition for a position perhaps to a public body such as a Borough Corporation, or to an institution such as the East India Company or the Customs and Excise, and this might well give biographical details including place of origin. Any application for a position with a private person or public institution whether for the advancement of one's career or financial assistance as with a pension or admission to an almshouse, might involve a petition and this again may give details of earlier career and origins.

Any position in the gift of a private person or of a manor, parish, borough, county, or of central government, may produce such a document and it should be sought amongst their surviving records. Some parish and county appointments, however, such as Parish Constables and High Constables did not normally require a formal application or petition, though they might be strengthened by a bond or surety and an oath - probably the Oath of Supremacy - would be taken before the Justices of the Peace.

F.2. Oaths

Under the Test Act of 1672 everyone appointed to public office had first to take the oaths of Allegiance and Supremacy and to provide proof of having taken the Sacrament of Communion of the Anglican Church. The 'Sacrament Certificate' was filed by the Justices of the Peace and provides the parish of residence. The office-holder might also make a Declaraction against Transubstantiation. All were designed to keep Roman Catholics from public office and were abolished in 1828, being replaced by a declaration which excluded Jews until 1860. Oaths of Office and Allegiance continue.

F.3. Government Employees

Such details as survive of Government employees are generally at the Public Record Office amongst the records of the appropriate department. It would seem that very few records give more than place of residence at the time of appointment. It was, of course, not customary to ask the age and place of birth of a gentleman who was generally accepted as such when appointing him to a government or any other office and such details are not recorded until the nineteenth century.

Those who had a patent of appointment would appear on the Patent Rolls in the Public Record Office, Chancery Lane, but (incomplete) calendars of these have only been published to the end of the reign of Queen Elizabeth I.

Lists of many officials have been published and there is a useful 'Biographical guide to the lists of English office-holders (to c.1800)' in the *Handbook of British chronology,* by F.M. Powicke and E.B. Fryde (Royal Historical Society, 1961). Annual lists are to be found in *Angliae notitia* (1669-1707), *Magnae Britanniae notitia* (1708-55), *The court and city register* (1742-1813), *The royal kalendar* (1767-1893) and other similar almanacs, precursors of *Whitaker's almanack* (first published in 1868). Some of these have consolidated indexes of names enabling an office- bearer to be traced from office to office throughout his lifetime.

Before 1855 government appointments were made upon the nomination of those in power but after that date they depended on the results of competitive examinations. The records remain with the Civil Service Department but the 'evidences of age' extracted from the case files of candidates for appointments, and usually consisting of a baptismal or birth certificate, have been deposited with the Society of Genealogists. The indexed series, which runs from 1855 to 1939, is unfortunately not complete.

An almanac similar to those mentioned above, *The British imperial calendar* (1810-72), developed into an official list of Civil Servants and was superseded by the *Civil service year-book* in 1873.

In 1972 the Institute of Historical Research began to publish a series of volumes listing *Office-holders in modern Britain* and have covered Treasury Officials 1660-1870 (vol. l, 1972), Officials of the Secretaries of State 1660-1782 (vol. 2, 1973), Officials of the Board of Trade 1660-1870 (vol. 3, 1974), Admiralty Officials 1660-1870 (vol. 4, 1975), Home Office Officials 1782-1870 (vol. 5, 1975), Colonial Office Officials 1794-1870 (vol. 6, 1976), Navy Board Officials 1660-1832 (vol. 7, 1978), Foreign Office Officials 1782-1870 (vol. 8, 1979) and Officials of Royal Commissions of Inquiry 1815-1870 (vol. 9, 1984). These include all grades, down to messengers and porters, and have useful introductory notes as to the methods of appointment used.

The official *Foreign Office List* was first published in 1852 and became the *Diplomatic Service List* in 1966. The earlier editions contain useful consolidated indexes of deaths covering long periods of years. The later editions generally give date of birth. The *Colonial Office List* was first published in 1862.

F.4. Royal Household

The names of members of the Royal Household may frequently be found in the almanacs listed above (**Section F.3.**). From these almanacs, from the warrants of appointments to the Household in the records of the Lord Chamberlain's Department 1641-1902 and the Lord Steward's Department 1598-1870 (now in the Public Record Office), and from the account books recording the establishment of particular households, an index has been compiled for the period 1660-1837. This is in the Royal Archives, Windsor Castle, Berkshire. The Royal Archives themselves contain no material prior to 1760. For additional sources prior to 1660 see the 'Biographical Guide to the Lists of English Office-Holders' mentioned in **Section F.2.** above.

F.5. Customs and Excise Officers

The principal officers of Customs (the customer or collector, the comptroller, and the searcher) were appointed by Letters Patent, the patentee often appointing a deputy by his own warrant. There are quarterly establishment records, showing the names, ranks, and ports, of all men employed by patent or warrant, with occasional gaps, from 1683 to 1829. They may be supplemented by records of oaths of office taken under departmental regulations or the Test Act, sureties given in the form of fidelity bonds (which may indicate family connections), and the 'Ages and Capacities' which give age. In the nineteenth century in some ports there are 'service records' giving details of all previous appointments.

The Establishment records for the Excise give much the same detail of quarterly salary lists, in various groups, from 1712 to 1835. The Minute Books of the Excise Board, 1696-1876, record the admission of entrants with their ages, their postings and transfers, and are indexed. They may also be supplemented by 'Ages and Capacity' records. From 1820 to 1870 the Entry Papers show parish of origin, parentage, sponsors or sureties, place of education and other details.

All the above records are now at the Public Record Office, Kew. See 'The Records of the Customs and the Excise Services' in *The genealogists' magazine*, vol. 10 (1948), pp. 219-25 and *Tracing your ancestors in the Public Record Office*, by A. Bevan and A. Duncan (4th edn. 1990), pp. 164-5.

The printed almanacs mentioned in **Section F.3.** above give, from 1691 onwards, the names of the principal officers of both Customs and Excise at headquarters, and in the case of the Customs those in the ports holding office by patent or warrant.

F.6. Policemen

A regular police force was established for the London area by the Metropolitan Police Act in 1829. It had authority within a twelve-mile radius of Charing Cross. The records, which show date and place of birth, are at the Public Record Office, Kew.

Within a few years forces had been established in other towns and then, in 1839 by the County Police Act, the Quarter Sessions in each county were empowered to appoint chief and petty constables, their appointment being made compulsory by the County and Borough Police Act in 1856. The records, which normally show date and place of birth, have usually been deposited in county record offices, but may remain with the local Police authority.

Sources for police history are described in L.A. Waters, *Police history monograph: notes for family historians* (Police History Society, 1987).

Prior to the above dates High or Chief Constables (as peace-keeping officers in the Hundred, previously appointed in the Hundred Court) and Petty or Parish Constables (who had similar duties within the parish) might be appointed by Quarter Sessions and the taking of their oath there recorded (*see above* **Section F.1.**). Both had administrative duties and appointments for those purposes continued to be made until about 1870.

F.7. Postmen

The records known as Nomination and Establishment of Employees, 1737- 1940 (indexed from 1830), show the appointments, places of employment and the transfers to other posts, of all grades of letter carriers, postmen, postmasters, clerks, labourers, and telegraphists employed by the Post Office. The Treasury Letters issued on retirement show the first and last positions held and sometimes the date of birth.

All these records are held at the Post Office Archives, Freeling House, Mount Pleasant, London EC1A 1BB, and are described in J. Farrugia, *A guide to the Post Office archives (London,* 1987).

F.8. Railwaymen

The staff registers of more than fifty of the old English and Welsh railway companies prior to nationalisation, commencing in 1835 and formerly at the British Rail Historical Records Department, are now at the Public Record Office, Kew. Their detail varies considerably from one company to another. Some list only names and rates of pay but others give considerable information including the date of birth, promotion and movement from one station to another (or to another railway company) of cleaners and clerks, firemen and engine drivers, apprentices, draughtsmen and station staff.

These records are described and listed in T. Richards, *Was your grandfather a railwayman?* (FFHS, 2nd edn. 1989).

With these records at the Public Record Office, Kew, are some relating to canals, docks, harbour navigation and steamship companies, generally with much less detail of staff.

G. PROFESSIONS

The movements of the professional classes may frequently be traced through the records of some central or qualifying body. The main records of the original professions, the church, law and medicine, may be summarised as follows:

G.1. Clergy

Some record of the ordination of priests and deacons may generally be found in the diocesan records of the appropriate bishop, and from 1716 the ordination papers normally include a baptismal certificate as proof of age. Institutions to benefices are recorded in the Bishops' Registers. Such records are deposited locally. See S. Bourne and A.H. Chicken, *Records of the Church of England: a practical guide for the family historian* (Maidstone, 1988).

The Clergy Institution Books at the Public Record Office, Chancery Lane, form a useful centralised record 1556-1838. They are arranged by county 1556-1660 or diocese 1661-1838, then by place, and show the name of the clergyman instituted, the date, and the name of the patron of the benefice. Although not showing any personal information they provide the outline of a career so that the clergyman can be traced from place to place.

Some clergy had a university degree and may thus be found in the printed university registers (*see above* **Section C.1. Schools and Universities**). The movements of clergy in the period 1800-40 may be found in the *Index ecclesiasticus,* by Joseph Foster (1890). There are printed *Clergy lists* from 1817 and *Crockford's clerical directory* has been published annually since 1858. The latter does not give date of birth (though modern editions may) or parentage, but notes the diocese in which ordination took place and sometimes the place of education.

For the diocese of London, G. Hennessy, *Novum repertorium ecclesiasticum parochiale Londinense: an ecclesiastical parochial history of the diocese of London* (London, 1898) is useful.

Curates had to be licensed by their bishops who required 'nominations' from the incumbents whose cures they were serving as well as proof of ordination. Files of nominations were kept in many dioceses, and from the early nineteenth century registers of licences were kept. In earlier times the licences might be entered in general licence books, with ordination records, or in subscription books. They are rarely complete.

Chaplains might, under Statute of Henry VIII, be appointed by archbishops, noblemen, some officers of state, and their widows, the certificates of appointment, dismissal or death, being recorded from 1660 in a series of books kept by the Faculty Office and now at Lambeth Palace Library.

G.2. Lawyers

Barristers were admitted through one of the four Inns of Court and the record of admittance shows age and the name and address of the father. The records of admissions have mostly been printed: Lincoln's Inn 1420- 1893, Middle Temple 15th century-1944, Inner Temple 1547-1660 only, and Grays Inn 1521-1889. Barristers only occasionally had a university degree. All judges were barristers.

Solicitors entered a five-year clerkship and their articles are filed chronologically from 1730 at the Public Record Office in the records of the Court of Common Pleas (1730-1838), the Court of King's Bench (1775- 1875), in some other courts, and from 1876 the Supreme Court. For details see *Tracing your ancestors in the Public Record Office,* by A. Bevan and A. Duncan (1990), pp. 176-80. They show the names and addresses of the fathers and there are manuscript indexes.

Other courts may contain similar records. Among the Durham Court of Chancery records of the Palatinate of Durham at The College, Durham DH1 3EQ, are two volumes of articles of clerkship, 1768-1875, providing the fathers' names.

Some attorneys served an apprenticeship and if the indentures were taxed would appear in the Apprentices of Great Britain 1710-74 (*see above* **Section C.2.**).

The printed annual *Law List* started in 1775, and although it shows the Inn of Court through which a barrister was admitted and the movement of a lawyer from one place to another, it does not show age or parentage.

An association of canon and civil lawyers who practised in the ecclesiastical courts and the Court of Admiralty originated in London at the end of the fifteenth century and was known as Doctors' Commons. It was dispersed in 1858 and its few surviving records are discussed in *Doctors' Commons,* by G.D. Squibb (1977).

G.3. Doctors

A physician or surgeon may have been apprenticed as mentioned above (**Section C.2.**), may have been licensed by a bishop or by the Dean of St Paul's (by an Act of 1511 which had fallen into disuse by the eighteenth century), may have had a degree in medicine from the Universities of Oxford or Cambridge or from the Scottish or Irish Universities or from one abroad such as Padua or Leyden, or had a degree from the Archbishop of Canterbury (from 1534), may have been a member of the Royal College of Physicians of London (in London from 1518 and nationally from 1522), may have been a member of the Barber-Surgeons Company in London (from 1540) or of one of the Barber Surgeons Companies in a provincial town, or of the Surgeons' Company in London (from 1745 to 1796), or of the Royal College of Surgeons of England (from 1800), or from 1617 have been a Licentiate of the Society of Apothecaries (which was national from 1815). Prior to 1617 an apothecary in London may have been a member of the Grocers' Company. All these records will normally show the name and address of the father.

Biographies of the Fellows of the Royal College of Physicians and of the Royal College of Surgeons have been published and there are printed annual *Medical directories* from 1845, *Medical registers* from 1859, and *Dentists registers* from 1888. These show places of education and qualification but not age or parentage. *Eighteenth century medics: a register,* by P.J. and R.V. Wallis (2nd edn. 1988) is valuable as an exhaustive name index to most published and unpublished sources for the period.

G.4. Other professions

During the nineteenth century there was a proliferation of central and qualifying bodies as the newer professions came into being and sought to organise themselves and impose standards on their members. Although their records may sometimes not give much more than age, many publish lists of their members which at least show their movements from place to place.

A list of such professional organisations is to be found in the *Directory of British associations* and of their publications in *Current British directories* (first published 1953). The libraries of professional bodies may contain greater detail and are listed in E.M. Codlin, *ASLIB directory of information sources in the United Kingdom* (2 vols., 6th edn. 1990) which has a subject index.

G.5. Trade and professional biographies

Biographical dictionaries of the members of many professions and of those who have practised certain trades have been published and may provide data not easily obtainable from other sources. The range is remarkable, including architects, artists, bell founders, clock and watch makers, engineers, furniture makers, gunsmiths, Members of Parliament, musicians, printers, sculptors, silversmiths and writers. Not all contain parental details or information on early life and education. Some, such as those for bookbinders and photographers, consist mainly of entries collected from trade directories but may indicate movement from place to place.

For a bibliography of such works see S. Raymond, *Occupational sources for genealogists* (FFHS, 1992).

G.6. Specialist trade indexes

Various specialist card indexes relating to particular trades are being built up by private family historians. They may, like directories, indicate movement from place to place. They include canal and river boatmen, Thames watermen and lightermen, coastguards, combmakers, glassmakers, gunmakers, lacemakers, lawyers, papermakers, proctors, shoemakers, tobacco pipe makers, woadpeople, etc. Full details and the charges involved in their consultation are given in J. Gibson and E. Hampson, *Marriage, census and other indexes for family historians* (FFHS, 4th edn. 1992).

H. ARMY AND NAVY

H.1. Army

The places of birth of most serving soldiers who died in service or were discharged to pension from 1732 onwards (from 1708 for the Artillery) may be found in the Muster Books in the War Office records at the Public Record Office at Kew, but very long searches may be involved if the regiment or campaign in which the man served is not known before 1883.

The Muster Books will enable any soldier, once his regiment is known, to be traced from place to place, so that his marriage or the baptisms of his children may be traced in local records.

From 1756 the Soldiers Documents, again arranged by Regiment to 1883, will provide an easier means of obtaining the age and place of birth of those discharged to pension.

The discharge certificates of those soldiers who remained in America (between 1776 and 1783) after the War of Independence unfortunately do not survive and so the information about the place of birth is lost, but the place of recruitment and the age at that time may be found.

From 1883 to 1913 the Soldiers Documents are arranged alphabetically in vast series covering the entire Army and so there is no need to know the regiment.

The service documents relating to the Boer War (1899-1902) are mostly lost. For the records of the First World War see the general books mentioned below and *World War I army ancestry* (FFHS, 1982) and *More sources of World War I army ancestry,* by N.W. Holding (FFHS, 1986)

Although the career details of Army officers can be found in the annual *Army List* from 1754 onwards, family details are not likely to be found before applications for commissions begin to be filed in the Commander-in-Chief's Memoranda in 1793, and not regularly until 1829 when the Return of Officers on Full-Pay gives date and place of birth. The Return of Half-Pay and Full-Pay Officers in 1828 merely shows date and place of marriage. There are, however, some birth certificates from 1755 onwards, all at the Public Record Office at Kew.

The applications for commissions in the Commander-in-Chief's Memoranda mentioned above may contain recommendations of friends and relatives for a commission with or without purchase, both perhaps giving details of place of residence and perhaps of other relatives in the same regiment.

Those who applied for cadetships at the Royal Military College (now Academy), Sandhurst (from 1812) and the Royal Military Academy, Woolwich (from 1880), provided age, and fathers' name and rank or occupation.

Details of earlier officers may be found in *English army lists and commission registers 1661-1714,* by Charles Dalton (London, 1892-1904) and the same author's *George the First's army 1714-1727* (London, 1910- 12). There is at the Public Record Office, Kew, a card index of the officers in the manuscript Army Lists 1702-1752.

The movements of retired officers may be traced from the quarterly statements of their addresses provided by the details of officers' pensions in the records of the Paymaster General's Office from 1737 onwards.

For army records generally see *My ancestor was in the British Army,* by M.J. and C.T. Watts (Society of Genealogists, 1992), *Army records for family historians,* by S. Fowler (PRO, 1992) and *Tracing your ancestors in the Public Record Office,* by A. Bevan and A. Duncan (London, 4th edn. 1990).

These books give details of the centralised militia records at the Public Record Office, but other militia records, particularly between 1757 and the end of the

Napoleonic Wars, may be found in some county record offices. Although these may not directly show place of origin, the returns of those liable for service are arranged by parish and provide valuable indications of age when men first appear (usually at the age of 18) or disappear (at 50 or, from 1763, at 45) from the record.

The Muster Rolls of Yeomanry and Volunteer Corps should also be found in county record offices from 1804 onwards showing the parish of origin.

For outline details of surviving militia records see J. Gibson and M. Medlycott, *Militia lists and musters 1757-1876: a directory of holdings in the British Isles* (FFHS, 1989).

H.2. Navy

The outline of the career of a commissioned officer can be constructed from the *Navy List,* published annually since 1782, and appears in *Commissioned sea officers of the Royal Navy,* 1660-1815 (National Maritime Museum, 3 vols. 1954). Further details, including sometimes parentage, may be found in *Biographia navalis; memoirs of the officers of the navy from 1600,* by John Charnock (4 vols. 1794-98), *Lives of British admirals,* by John Campbell (4 vols. 1779), and *Royal naval biography,* by John Marshall, covering all officers who had reached the rank of commander and who were living or had recently died at the time of publication (12 vols. 1823-30; typescript index of names at Society of Genealogists).

The *Navy List* also gives seniority and disposition lists of Masters, Pursers, Surgeons, Chaplains, Yard Officers, and officers serving in the Coastguard, Revenue Cruisers and packets.

The *Naval biographical dictionary,* by W.R. O'Byrne (London, 1849) includes every officer of the rank of lieutenant and above, serving or retired, and alive in 1845. Frequently the fathers and other serving relatives are mentioned. The original manuscript for the book, which often gives additional details, is in the Manuscripts Department of the British Library (Add.MS. 38039-54).

The Lieutenants' Passing Certificates 1691-1902, at the Public Record Office at Kew, give the candidate's previous career, and from 1789 (with a few from 1777) have filed with them baptismal certificates as proof of age. Indexes of the latter are available to 1832. Where the certificate is missing the place of birth can be found from the muster roll of any ship in which the ancestor served before his promotion to lieutenant.

Prior to 1853 the place of birth of an ordinary seaman can only be discovered if the name of any ship on which he served is known. That may be found from the Medal Rolls 1793-1914 if a campaign or battle is known, or from the List Books 1673-1893 if the place of his service at a particular time is known.

If the name of a ship is known the Ships Musters 1667-1878 should provide age and place of birth. If superannuated after 1802 a complete service record will be found in the Warrant Officers' and Seamens' Services 1802-71.

After 1853 men entering the service were assigned a Continuous Service Number and the Engagement Books 1853-72 and Registers of Services 1873-91 include their dates and places of birth.

There is a great variety of naval records at the Public Record Office and in addition to those mentioned above others, such as Pensions, Bounty Papers and Effects Papers, may contain details of age, place of origin and relationships. For naval records generally see *Tracing your ancestors in the Public Record Office,* by A. Bevan and A. Duncan (London, 4th edn. 1990) and *Naval records for genealogists,* by N.A.M. Rodger (London, 1988).

H.3. Merchant Seamen

There are few records before 1835. The Registers of Seamen are in four overlapping, mainly alphabetical series, 1835-57, and give age and place of birth. They refer to Crew lists which give similar information as well as additional details of careers. Crew lists, 1857-1938, are scattered in various repositories, but cannot be used until the name of a ship is known as there are no indexes of names.

An index of indentured apprentices, 1824-1953, gives age at apprenticeship but the indentures themselves only survive for every fifth year after 1845.

The Registers of Certificates of Competency for Masters and Mates, from 1844, give date and place of birth. From 1857 their names are published annually in the *Mercantile navy list.* All the above records are at the Public Record Office at Kew.

Lloyd's captains' register giving complete career details for all Masters and their dates and places of birth was published only once in 1869 (reprinted in 1986 on microfiche by the Society of Genealogists) but an annual manuscript continuation to 1948 exists at the Guildhall Library, London.

From the sixteenth century to 1854 the Corporation of Trinity House, London, frequently assisted merchant seamen and their dependants who had fallen on hard times. The surviving records, now deposited with the Society of Genealogists, date from about 1750 to 1890. They consist mainly of petitions sent in by distressed seamen, their widows (or the wives of those imprisoned in France) and children between 1787 and 1854 with supporting documents and certificates, but there are smaller groups of apprenticeship indentures of seamen 1818-45 and other documents in connection with almshouse applications 1790-90. There is a full calendar and index in *The Trinity House Petitions* (Society of Genealogists, 1987).

For further details of sources see *My ancestor was a merchant seaman: how can I find out more about him?*, by C.T. and M.J. Watts (Society of Genealogists, 2nd edn. 1991).

H.4. Marines

Records of Officers' Services commence in 1793 but are not complete until about 1837. They show age and place of origin, and occasionally the name and profession of the father.

For records of other ranks one needs to know the division or company, or else a search through each in turn will be needed. However, the Description Books, from about 1750, give by date of enlistment, the age and place of birth. From 1790 the Attestation Forms, completed on enlistment, are arranged by date of discharge, then by division and initial letter of surname, and provide details of service.

Most records are at the Public Record Office at Kew. See *Tracing your ancestors at the Public Record Office,* by A. Bevan and A. Duncan (London, 4th edn. 1990).

H.5. Coastguards

The Coastguard was founded in 1822, its Officers and many of the men coming from the Royal Navy. The Establishment Books 1816-1923 and Muster Books 1824-57 are indexed by station and there are some nominal indexes to the Registers of Nominations for Appointments 1819-66, all at the Public Record Office at Kew. Those recruited from the Merchant Navy may be traced to their places of birth through the Registers of Seamen 1835-57. The Officers are listed in the *Navy list.*

I. LAND OWNERSHIP

I.1. Copyhold Land

The clues to origins that may be found in wills have been considered above (*see* **Section B.4.**). In addition a bequest of copyhold land (i.e. land held by copy of an entry on a manor court roll) may be particularly helpful as the manor records will show how and when it was obtained. Customary tenures on English manors were administered by the court baron and changes in tenancy could only be made by surrender and admission in the court. Most manorial books are indexed after about 1650. If there is no index the entry of the 'surrender' of the property to the uses of the will (made at the time of probate) will refer back to the date of its purchase or receipt by inheritance and the entry at that time will repeat the procedure. The system continued in some manors until 1922.

For the whereabouts of manorial records consult the Register of Manorial Documents maintained by the Historical Manuscripts Commission, Quality House, Quality Court, Chancery Lane, London WC2A 1HP. For general descriptions of manorial records see *Manorial records,* by P.D.A. Harvey (London, 1984) and *My ancestors were manorial tenants,* by P.B. Park (Society of Genealogists, 2nd edn. 1994).

I.2. Boroughs

In London and most corporate towns there was a customary right to bequeath land by will and the registration of deeds was fairly common. Such records, which are less common after the Commonwealth period but may revive later, remain with the borough records. The receipt of property by bequest, however, is more often revealed by searching for earlier wills of the same surname (through the local probate courts and the Prerogative Court of Canterbury) than through records of this kind.

I.3. Deeds

There was no general registration of freehold land in England or Wales prior to the nineteenth century except (as mentioned above) in certain boroughs and (as mentioned below) in Middlesex and Yorkshire. It is still far from complete in rural areas. Deeds were not required to be kept and survive only haphazardly. Land ownership and transfer is thus frequently extremely difficult to trace. If the migrant possessed land, however, the possibility of surviving deeds which might hold some clue to his place of origin should always be investigated.

There are miscellaneous collections of deeds in most county record offices and there are large groups of deeds in the Public Record Office but many are calendared, if at all, by place and not by name.

Conveyances of freehold property by gift, bequest, sale or mortgage have been registered in Middlesex (from 1708) and Yorkshire (West Riding from 1704, East Riding from 1707, and North Riding from 1735) and are a valuable source of information about those who purchased property in those counties. The records are deposited in the appropriate county record offices. See 'The Deeds Registries of Yorkshire and Middlesex', by F. Sheppard and V. Belcher in *Journal of the Society of Archivists,* vol. 2 (1980), pp. 274-86.

For a general survey of records of this kind see *Sources for the history of houses,* by J.H. Harvey (1974), *Old title deeds,* by N.W. Alcock (1986) and *Title deeds,* by A.A. Dibben (1990).

The registration of land in Ireland and Scotland is of great importance for the genealogist but is beyond the scope of this booklet. It should be noted that the granting by the Crown of land in Ireland and the Colonies rarely indicates the place of origin in England of the grantee.

I.4. Poll Books and Registers of Electors

Between 1694 and 1868 when the right to vote (except in the boroughs) was based mainly on ownership of freehold land (before 1832 the ownership of land worth 40s a year), the poll books giving the names of those who voted at elections will show the addresses of those who lived away from the parish in which their freehold lay. Similarly, non-resident freemen are listed separately in the polls of freemen boroughs. This is a useful indication of movement and should be investigated. As the poll may also show occupiers of property who did not themselves own land, the places of abode of their landlords may occasionally give indications of the tenants' places of origin.

Many polls have been printed but some unpublished polls remain in county record Offices. The *Handlist of British parliamentary poll books,* by J. Sims (University of Leicester, 1984) and *Poll books c.1696-1872: a directory to holdings in Great Britain,* by J. Gibson and C. Rogers (FFHS, 1989) indicate where surviving printed copies may be found. Those at the Society of Genealogists, where there is a useful consolidated index to forty-one printed polls, 1702-1807, are listed in *Directories and poll books in the possession of the Society of Genealogists* (Society of Genealogists, 5th edn. 1989).

The Registers of Electors which were printed annually in most counties after the Reform Act of 1832 continue to give their places of residence as well as the situation of the properties in respect of which they voted. As late as the First World War the printed *Absent voters' lists* form a record of men serving in the Forces and will show by parish their service identification. For the whereabouts of surviving copies see *Electoral registers since 1832: and burgess rolls,* by J. Gibson and C. Rogers (FFHS, 1989).

I.5. Jurors' Lists

From 1696 the constables of the parishes were required to send to Quarter Sessions lists of those eligible for jury service, i.e. those having a freehold or copyhold worth £10 a year who were aged between 21 and 70. The property qualification was increased in 1825 when the qualifying age was reduced to 60. The records survive reasonably well in many county record offices and may provide a useful indication of age in the absence of an age at burial.

I.6. Certificates of Residence

Although a little early for the purposes of this booklet the Certificates of Residence from c.1546 to c.1660 in the Exchequer records at the Public Record Office, Chancery Lane, afford valuable evidence of change of residence. Formerly attached to the Lay Subsidy Returns they certify that the persons named had paid a particular tax in one county and were not liable in another. There is an alphabetical list by surname, forename, county and regnal year.

J. COURT DEPOSITIONS

A man did not need to own land to make a deposition as a witness or to be a plaintiff in court proceedings but the information provided may give clues to earlier history or family connections. In some courts a deposition may include some statement of age and place of origin. Unfortunately the great majority of court proceedings are merely indexed, if at all, by the plaintiff's name.

J.1. Chancery and Exchequer Courts

Particularly important in this context are the records of the Courts of Chancery and the Exchequer. There are indexes to Chancery deponents, 1534-1800, and plaintiffs 1714-1800, and to Exchequer deponents, 1559-1800, in the Bernau Index at the Society of Genealogists, the records themselves being at the Public Record Office, Chancery Lane. The Index, which is on microfilm and contains over four million entries, rarely gives any indication of place of residence and the identification of particular persons may be a lengthy task. From the genealogical point of view the three typescript volumes of *Indexes to disputed estates in Chancery 1649-1714*, by P.W. Coldham are particularly useful.

Other indexes are listed in *Tracing your ancestors in the Public Record Office*, by A. Bevan and A. Duncan (4th edn. 1990) and in 'Genealogical Resources in Chancery Records', by P.W. Coldham in *The genealogists' magazine*, vol. 19 (1979), pp. 345-7. For a general account see *Chancery and other legal proceedings*, by R.E.F. Garrett (1968).

J.2. Ecclesiastical Courts

The personal details of those who gave evidence in the local ecclesiastical courts probably form one of the largest bodies of information about the ages and places of origin of people in England yet to be explored by genealogists. The importance of these courts, however, declined considerably in the course of the seventeenth century. The records would be with the other diocesan records, usually in the appropriate county record office. Very few have been calendared and speculative searches would be lengthy. For an example see *Winchester Consistory Court depositions 1561-1602*, by A.J. Willis (1960). A valuable index to the depositions in the Court of Arches, the Court of Appeal for the Province of Canterbury, is to be found in *Index of cases in the records of the Court of Arches at Lambeth Palace Library 1660-1913*, by Jane Houston (Index Library, vol. 85, 1972).

J.3. Other Courts

The depositions at Assizes, where they have survived, show place of residence and sometimes age, but not place of origin, and are poorly calendared, thus 'a speculative search', as *Tracing your ancestors in the Public Record Office* used to say, 'is ill advised'. There is a similar lack of information about those who came before Quarter Sessions, their ages not normally being given, though the records of these and other local courts may generally be better calendared. The few surviving depositions in the Court of Chivalry, mainly dealing with the unlawful use of Arms and therefore more likely to contain direct genealogical information, are calendared in *Reports of heraldic cases in the Court of Chivalry 1623-1732*, by G.D. Squibb (Harleian Society, vol. 107, 1956).

J.4. Criminals

Details of a defendant in a criminal case are often rather disappointing. They frequently do not give more than the place of residence and occupation at the time of being 'taken up', though in the nineteenth century the age may appear.

All those convicted of indictable offences in London and Middlesex from 1791, and for the rest of England and Wales from 1805, are indexed in the Annual Criminal Registers at the Public Record Office, Kew, which show where their trials took place. Those for Middlesex show age, and occasionally, place of birth. The Calendars of Prisoners in the Public Record Office, Kew, or in the appropriate county record office, and the Prison Registers in the Public Record Office, Kew, usually show age and other personal details. The petitions from criminals and their families at the Public Record Office, 1762-1871, may provide other biographical data.

For examples of these records see *Criminal ancestors,* by D.T. Hawkings (1992) and *Bound for Australia,* by D.T. Hawkings (1987).

A contemporary newspaper account may give more detail about a criminal than the surviving court records and the possibilities should always be investigated. For newspapers *see above* **Section B.6.** The charge for returning persons discharged from prison to their places of settlement fell on Quarter Sessions and would be there recorded but the names of individuals are not always given.

K. RELIEF OF THE POOR

K.1. Settlement Certificates

From the early seventeenth century parish authorities, who from 1601 onwards had a statutory duty to maintain the poor and provide them with work, viewed with the greatest suspicion the arrival of a new man, with or without a family, particularly if it looked as though he would not be able to support himself and might then become a charge on the parish.

By an Act of 1662 the parish authorities (the Overseers of the Poor appointed under the 1601 Act and the Churchwardens) could send away a stranger unless he was able to rent a property to the value of £10 or more. The pauper was first examined by local Justices of the Peace to determine his place of settlement. The ages of any children were recorded. The physical removal of the family could not, however, take place until it became chargeable to the parish.

The cost of the removal by the overseers would be entered in their account books which, with any examination record, would be kept in the parish chest. If there was an appeal or a dispute with the parish to which the stranger was returned, which there frequently was, this would be heard by the Justices in Quarter Sessions and there recorded.

A further Act of 1697 allowed the new parish to which a person went to ask that he brought with him from his own parish a certificate that he was settled there and that that parish would receive him back again if he fell on hard times. These Settlement Certificates were carefully kept in the parish chest as the authority for returning a man. Together with declarations of personal circumstances and the results of examinations they may be entered into special books kept for that purpose. Some county record offices have made composite indexes of settlement papers for their counties.

A man's place of settlement was normally his place of birth, but settlement might be acquired by renting a separate and distinct building of an annual rental of at least £10, or by the payment of taxes and dues on property of an annual value of at least £10, or by apprenticeship by indenture in another parish, or by hiring for service for a full year to the same man in another parish, whichever happened most recently.

Such matters were frequently disputed and although the original settlement papers may long since have been destroyed some record may be found, as mentioned above, in the appropriate Quarter Sessions records. A dispute may be taken to a higher court such as King's Bench. For the cases heard there, 1732-76, see *A series of the decisions of the Court of King's Bench upon settlement, 1732-1776*, by James Burrow (2 vols. 1768-82).

The system remained in force until 1876 and the passing of the Divided Parishes and Poor Law Amendment Act that year. Although it mainly applied to the poorer classes it is unwise to assume that one's ancestors will not appear or that the record has not survived merely because nothing can be found in the parish records. The Quarter Sessions records must be searched.

For a general description of settlement records see *The parish chest,* by W.E. Tate (1967).

K.2. Vagrants

Houses of Correction for rogues and vagabonds, under the supervision of the Justices, were established in the sixteenth century, and orders about them may be found until 1834 in Quarter Session Records, though independent records of their inmates prior to the mid-eighteenth century seem rarely to survive.

From 1699 there were fixed rates of payment for the conveyancing of vagrants to their places of settlement and contracts for the work might be entered into. The contractors would keep lists (rarely surviving) of the vagrants passed and the Justices would file orders for their removal and passing with details of payments and of rewards given for their apprehension.

In some areas by Act of 1833 arrangements were made with shipping companies for the conveyance of vagrants to Ireland and Scotland. In London the examinations of Irish and Scottish paupers removed from the City and showing their places of birth survive at the Guildhall Library from 1834 to 1846. In some places an end seems to have been put to such schemes by the 1834 Act.

The attempts of individual parishes through their overseers of the poor and local constables to punish and remove vagabonds may also be found recorded with their attendant expenses in their account books. Stray entries of removals are frequently found entered in parish registers.

K.3. Long distance apprenticeship of pauper children

As mentioned above in **Section C.2.** indentures of pauper children placed as apprentices by the Overseers of the Poor sometimes survive and registers were sometimes kept.

Large numbers of poor, orphaned or abandoned children were sent to work as apprentices in the textile mills of the industrial north during the late eighteenth and early nineteenth centuries. From about 1786 children were sent from London parishes to Lancashire, Cheshire, Nottinghamshire and Derbyshire, and by 1805 to Glasgow, to work in the cotton, woollen, worsted and silk milling areas. Some were bound out from the age of eight until they were twenty-one. Their numbers declined following the 1802 Health and Morals of Apprentices Act and in 1816 an Act restricted the distance to which they could be sent to a forty-mile radius of London.

The registers of these apprentices were kept by the home parishes. They are described by Pamela Horn in 'The traffic in children and the textile mills 1780-1816' in *The genealogists' magazine,* vol. 24 (1993), pp. 177-85.

K.4. Workhouses and Boards of Guardians

Parishes, whether individually or in union with others, were encouraged to keep workhouses by an Act of 1722 and by Gilbert's Act of 1782. Records of the inmates rarely survive but would be with the parish records and may show age and place of origin and/or settlement.

The Poor Law Reform Act of 1834 established Unions of parishes on a statutory basis and appointed Boards of Guardians to administer them. Their voluminous records are in the appropriate county record offices though the Unions were established without regard to county boundaries. They are supplemented by the Poor Law Union Papers, 1834-1900, in the Public Record Office, Kew.

The Guardians were responsible for all aspects of poor relief. They gave assistance to those who were incapable of work or temporarily ill either in or out of the workhouse, apprenticed pauper children, took care of those children who were abandoned or left orphans, and through the workhouse hospital tended those who were chronically sick or dying. Some Boards sponsored schemes to send pauper workers to more prosperous areas of the country (particularly from Suffolk, Norfolk, Bedfordshire and Buckinghamshire to the mills of Lancashire, Yorkshire, Cheshire and Derbyshire in the period 1835-43) or to Australia or Canada. In every case the age and place of settlement or origin of those who were relieved was recorded.

The system was not entirely abolished until the reforms of 1946-8 when the medical duties passed to the Ministry of Health working through Hospital Boards, the local authorities remaining responsible for children and old people.

For examples of the records see *Handlist of the records of the Board of Guardians in the county of Somerset,* by H. King (1949) and for the whereabouts of such records generally see *Poor law union records,* by J. Gibson, C. Rogers and C. Webb (FFHS, 4 parts, 1993) the fourth part of which is a valuable gazetteer of the parishes in each union.

Asylums for pauper lunatics might be established under an Act of 1808. They were administered by Quarter Sessions and from 1834 by the Boards of Guardians. Their records show age and place of origin.

K.5. Hospitals

Speculative searches in hospital records are rarely worthwhile unless a birth or death took place in a known hospital. In the majority of hospitals records rarely go back beyond the beginning of the twentieth century, and public access is not allowed until they are more than one hundred years old.

However, admission registers may survive from earlier times, as at the Middlesex Hospital from 1745 and at Manchester from 1752, showing the patient's normal place of residence. The admission registers of lying-in hospitals, like the British Lying-in Hospital, Holborn, which catered for the poor wives of soldiers and sailors from 1749 to 1868, always show the place of settlement of the mother.

Hospital death registers, particularly after 1837, show the home address of the patient, something rarely indicated on the early death certificates of those who died in hospital.

Full details of all hospital records held in public repositories are contained in the Hospital Records Project computer database at the Public Record Office, Kew.

L. RELIGION

Clergy of the Church of England are not well known for keeping detailed registers of the membership of their congregations. They kept registers of their baptisms, marriages and burials, and occasionally of those confirmed, but only rarely did they maintain any register showing from whence newcomers came and the destinations of those who left. In the nineteenth century some maintained 'visiting lists' and other memoranda about their parishioners which may include these details. Such registers are, however, quite frequently found of nonconformist congregations.

L.1. Presbyterians, Independents, Baptists

The Presbyterians, Independents or Congregationalists and the Baptists often kept Church Rolls of their members, showing their names, addresses, and the date of their admission to membership. They are less likely to record the date of their removal by death, erasure or transfer. Entries of this kind are sometimes found in the church Minute Book. The bringing of a letter from the minister of the chapel one previously attended might also be recorded. If they survive these records are to be found at the chapel or at the local county record office.

The registers of baptisms and burials in these congregation prior to 1837, are usually in the Public Record Office, Chancery Lane, with other 'Non-Parochial Registers'. Those which have been deposited there are indexed in the International Genealogical Index (1993 edition).

Also deposited at the Public Record Office, Chancery Lane, is Dr. Williams' General Register of Nonconformist births, 1742-1837, a centralised index to the births of many Baptists, Independents and Presbyterians which should not be overlooked. Some retrospective entries date from 1716. The entries, which were sent in from all over the British Isles and include many births overseas, are not as yet included in the International Genealogical Index. *See also* **Section L.5.** *below.*

The obituary notices of nonconformist ministers and prominent laymen, found in the Magazines and Year Books of the various denominations, may give details of age, education and early origins.

For further detail see *My ancestors were Baptists,* by G.R. Breed (Society of Genealogists, 2nd edn. 1994), *My ancestors were Congregationalists,* by D.J.H. Clifford (Society of Genealogists, 1992) and *My ancestors were English Presbyterians/Unitarians,* by A. Ruston (Society of Genealogists, 1993) and *National index of parish registers,* vol. 2 (1973), pp. 574-5.

L.2. Methodists

Membership of the Methodist Church involved from its commencement enrolment in the class list of a leader, one or more of which might form a church or society. Membership Rolls for the Circuit were also compiled.

The registers of baptisms and burials in these congregations prior to 1837, are usually in the Public Record Office, Chancery Lane, with other 'Non-Parochial Registers'. Those which have been deposited there are indexed in the International Genealogical Index (1993 edition).

The registers of the central Metropolitan Wesleyan Registry in Paternoster Row, London, 1818-41, also deposited at the Public Record Office, Chancery Lane, form a centralised index to many Wesleyan births and should not be overlooked. The entries are not as yet included in the International Genealogical Index.

Obituary notices of Wesleyan ministers and prominent laymen, which may give details of age, education and early origins, are to be found in a variety of journals and there are indexes to many in the Methodist Connexional Archives. Lists of most ministers and their circuits have been published.

For further details see *My ancestors were Methodists,* by W. Leary (Society of Genealogists, 2nd edn. 1990), *National index of parish registers,* vol. 2 (London and Chichester, 1973), pp. 733-5, and *How to write a local history of Methodism,* by W.F. Swift (1981), pp. 13-4.

L.3. Quakers

In the Society of Friends (Quakers) it had become customary from the 1670s for Friends moving from one monthly meeting to another to carry with them a certificate. From the mid-eighteenth century it became general to record outgoing certificates and in many cases incoming certificates were kept on file. There are, however, few registers of members before 1812, though they are in general use from 1837. The majority of these records are in the appropriate county record offices.

Register books of births, marriages and burials began to be kept by Quaker meetings from the late 1650s (with some retrospective entries to 1578). When they were surrendered in the 1840s and in 1857 digests were made and retained by the Society of Friends. These digests, now at Friends House Library, Euston Road, London NW1 2BJ, form useful centralised indexes to the registers which are not, as yet, indexed into the International Genealogical Index (1993 edn.).

For further details see *My ancestors were Quakers,* by E.H. Milligan and M.J. Thomas (Society of Genealogists, 1983).

L.4. Catholics

The few Catholic registers deposited at the Public Record Office, Chancery Lane, are indexed in the International Genealogical Index (1993 edition) but the majority were not deposited. All known registers are listed in *Catholic missions and registers 1700-1880,* by M.J. Gandy (London, 6 vols., 1993).

The listing of Catholics on the Recusant Rolls and the registration of their estates may provide some assistance in tracing them from place to place. Their records generally are described in D.J. Steel, *National index of parish registers: sources for Roman Catholic genealogy and family history* (London and Chichester, vol. 3, 1974). *See also* **Section L.5.** *below.*

L.5. General Registry of Births at College of Arms

In 1747 a General Registry of Births of people not baptised in the Established Church was established at the College of Arms and registered a few hundred events ranging in date from 1734 to 1793 mostly relating to Jews, Moravians and Roman Catholics, but including a few other dissenters. The records remain at the College and are not included in the International Genealogical Index. There are some abstracts and a complete index of surnames in the article 'The General Registry of Births at the Heralds' College', by D.J. Steel in *National index of parish registers,* vol. 3 (London and Chichester, 1974), pp. 981-98.

L.6. General Comment

Because of their particular belief members of these and other smaller religious groups sought out like-minded people in the areas to which they came. In searching for their origins the International Genealogical Index (*see above* **Section A.3.**) is now particularly helpful, indexing, as it does, all the individual registers of baptism at the Public Record Office. The omissions mentioned above should, however, be noted. Such registers vary greatly in the amount of information included; they should thus be searched over wide periods and the burial registers also consulted.

It should never be assumed that a family remained firmly attached to a particular belief. Movements from one type of congregation to another over a wide area of religious belief are frequently met with, particularly in the early nineteenth century. Few families have 'always been staunch Anglicans' despite family traditions to that effect.

For the whole range of nonconformist records see the *National index of parish registers,* by D.J. Steel: vol. 2 *Sources for nonconformist genealogy and family history* (London and Chichester, 1973), and vol. 3 *Sources for Roman Catholic (and Jewish) genealogy and family history* (London and Chichester, 1974).

M. NAMES

M.1. Distinctive Forenames

If the migrant had a distinctive forename, whether or not it was carried down in his family, this may be an indication of a place of origin or ancestry if it can be found in earlier families of the name in the same or lower social class. Indexes which cover a wide area and give numerous examples should be searched for such occurrences, e.g. the International Genealogical Index, Boyd's Marriage Index, the Apprenticeship Index 1710-74, the Great Card Index of the Society of Genealogists, and the large printed indexes such as those of the Prerogative Court of Canterbury Wills and Musgrave's Obituary.

If the migrant or one of his children has a forename which seems likely to be a surname given perhaps at baptism to perpetuate a connection with some other family, a possible ancestral marriage between the two families must be sought, again through such indexes as the International Genealogical Index or Boyd's Marriage Index or some local marriage index. Such a name may come not only from a mother or grandmother, but also from an uncle by marriage. It may, however, sometimes come from an unrelated god-parent, but in England some family relationship is usually found.

Some rare forenames are found in particular parts of the country and their use may thus indicate a possible area of origin. The comments in the *Oxford dictionary of English christian names,* by E.G. Withycombe (1950) may then be helpful.

M.2. Distribution of Surname

If the surname of the migrant is sufficiently uncommon a general search for other occurrences in the immediate area should be undertaken. This has sometimes to be slowly expanded and a general search made. Such a 'one-name study' may, in extreme cases, be the only answer, particularly where the movement has been to another country, as from England to Ireland or America. Surnames on which such studies are currently being made may be found in the *Register of one-name studies* (Guild of One-Name Studies, 9th edn. 1992).

Some indication of the general distribution of a name may be obtained from *The homes of family names in Great Britain,* by H.B. Guppy (1890, reprinted 1968) and, because of its references to the *Return of owners of land 1873,* from *A dictionary of English and Welsh surnames,* by C.W. Bardsley (1901). The derivations of names in the latter, it should be added, are frequently suspect.

As with distinctive forenames, indexes with a wide coverage will need to be searched, e.g. the International Genealogical Index, Boyd's Marriage Index, and the Great Card Index at the Society of Genealogists. A standard approach is to extract all the wills of persons of the same surname in the immediate area, and in increasing circles, both before and after migration, in the hope that the will of the father or of some other relation may be found which mentions the migrant, his property, or some known member of his family. With a migrant abroad this is usually first done by searching the wills proved in the Prerogative Court of Canterbury and then those proved in the local courts of the areas in which the surname is found. If the migration was before 1700 a preliminary survey of the printed indexes of these wills published by the British Record Society in its Index Library series will quickly show whether such an approach is likely to be feasible. It is recommended homework for any searcher for the origin of an American immigrant in the seventeenth century!

M.3. Aliases

Prior to about 1730 the use of an alias nearly always indicates that two surnames have developed for the same family, one perhaps being descriptive of their place of residence and the other of their trade, some people perhaps knowing them by the first and others by the second. That being the case the use of both names together will be found back to the sixteenth century or earlier and should be searched for in the records giving wide coverage mentioned in the last Section. Later such an alias may indicate illegitimacy or adoption.

M.4. Changes of Name

Many changes of name go unrecorded and children frequently take their stepfathers' names for convenience sake, making searches for their origins difficult. Change of name needs no legal formality but most changes of name by Deed Poll, Royal Licence and Act of Parliament are indexed in W.P.W. Phillimore and E.A. Fry, *An index to changes of name 1760-1901* (London, 1905) which shows both the new and the old name.

N. COATS OF ARMS

If a man appears to have used a coat of arms or a crest, perhaps on a bookplate, when sealing his will, or on his monument, tombstone or hatchment, the arms themselves may give an indication of uncertain value of the claimed place of origin of his family even if he had no right to the arms. The use of a quartered coat, suggesting a possible ancestral marriage which might be searched for, may be more helpful. The arms and quarterings may be identified through *Papworth's ordinary of British armorials,* by J.W. Papworth (London, 1874, reprinted 1961).

The unlawful assumption of arms has, of course, been known since at least the sixteenth century but became epidemic in the nineteenth century when practically every person with any pretensions to social standing assumed arms, taking the details (or being provided with them by an heraldic stationer) from printed armories such as the *General armory,* by Sir Bernard Burke (London, 1884, reprinted 1976) which had become widely available.

The great majority of arms granted between 1687 and 1898 with a great number from the fifteenth century are listed in *Grantees of arms,* by J. Foster (Harleian Society, vols. 66-68, 1915-7). The grant itself may indicate origin or a pedigree may have been registered at the time or subsequently, both at the College of Arms.

If a family lawfully used arms in England between 1530 and 1687 its pedigree is likely to have been recorded at one of the Heralds' Visitations taken periodically throughout that period. Many of these have been printed and references to the families will therefore be found in the bibliographies of printed pedigrees mentioned below (**Section O.1.**). To find whether the arms of any particular family appear in a printed version of a visitation see *Index to the quartered coats of arms in the Harleian Society Visitation Series* (1961) and *Index to coats of arms from various sources not included in the Index to the Harleian Visitation Series* (1962), both by Professor R.C. Gale.

If a family improperly used arms in the period 1623-1732 some details may be found in the published records of the Court of Chivalry (Harleian Society, vol. 107, 1956).

If a family used arms after 1687 and there is no grant or pedigree recorded at the College of Arms it may be useful to see what other families of the name used the arms in an earlier period. This again can be done by using the bibliographies of printed pedigrees mentioned below. Searches may then be made in that area, but the temptation to trace the descendants of a lawfully armigerous family of the same surname just because their arms were used by a family in the nineteenth century should generally be firmly resisted. It is because the origin of the later family cannot be found in the family and area from which tradition says it came that one should be searching for it elsewhere.

O. HAS WORK BEEN DONE BEFORE?

In cases where a family appears in a particular place and its earlier history is unknown the possibility of work having been done by others on the earlier history should be investigated.

O.1. Printed Pedigrees

Any account containing more than three generations of a family which has appeared in print should be indexed in either *The genealogist's guide,* by G.W. Marshall (London, 1903, reprinted Baltimore, 1967), or *A genealogical guide,* by J.B. Whitmore (London, 1953), or *The genealogist's guide,* by G.B. Barrow (London and Chicago, 1977), or in their addenda and corrigenda. The Supplement to *A catalogue of British family histories,* by T.R. Thomson (3rd edn. London, 1980) contains additional references to material published in the period 1975-80. All must be consulted and all the references, however unlikely they may appear, must be checked.

For Scotland consult also *Scottish family history,* by M. Stuart (Edinburgh, 1930) and its continuation *Scottish family histories,* by J. Ferguson (Edinburgh, 1986).

For Ireland consult the *Bibliography of Irish family history and genealogy,* by B. de Breffny (Cork, 1974) and the less complete but more up to date *Bibliography of Irish family history,* by E. MacLysaght (Dublin, 1982).

O.2. Manuscript Pedigrees

If a manuscript pedigree survives it may be almost anywhere as many genealogists have not yet learned to place copies of their material in the library of the Society of Genealogists, but check the Document Collection of the Society, the Family History section of the Library Catalogue, and its Index of Pedigrees in Deposited Collections. There may be a pedigree in the library of the local Family History Society or deposited with the appropriate county record office.

For the material on gentry families prior to about 1700 in the Manuscripts Department of the British Library consult *An index to the pedigrees and arms contained in the heralds' visitations and other genealogical manuscripts in the British Museum,* by R. Sims (London, 1849).

There may be a pedigree registered at the College of Arms but there is no published list of the pedigrees there, though a Grant of Arms (*see* **Section N.**) may suggest that a pedigree was registered at the same time. Pedigrees registered at the time of the Heralds' Visitations between 1530 and 1687 may also survive in copies at the British Library (*see above*) and/or have been printed (*see* **Section O.1.**).

O.3. One-Name Studies

If a one-name study is being carried out the *Register of one-name studies* (9th edn. London, 1992) published by the Guild of One-Name Studies, and containing about fifteen-hundred entries will provide the details. *See also* **Section M.2. Distribution of Surname.**

O.4. Interests

For the names and addresses of other persons who may be working on the same ancestors consult the *National genealogical directory,* by M.J. Burchall (7 vols., Brighton, 1979-86) and I. Caley (7 vols., Ringmer, 1987-93), the *Genealogical research directory,* by K.A. Johnson and M.R. Sainty (12 vols., London, 1982-93), and *The ancestral file* published yearly on microfiche by the Genealogical Society of Utah. Many local Family History Societies also publish lists of their members' interests. There is a card index of the interests of the members of the Society of Genealogists at the Society into which has been filed the former 'National Pedigree Index'.

O.5. General Comment

It is a mistake to accept some family tradition of a descent from a famous person in the past and to trace all his/her descendants in the happy thought that one will be amongst them. The temptation to reject the first rule in all genealogical work, i.e. of working from the known to the unknown, should generally be firmly rejected. Only when the name is very rare will speculative searches prove worthwhile.

P. STRAYS

In recent years with the growth of local Family History Societies there has been a move to index entries of persons found recorded in unlikely places and away from their normal places of residence and entries which show origins in a county other than that of residence. Many such entries have been published in the journals of local societies and some societies have appointed 'strays co-ordinators' and hold considerable 'indexes of strays'. Some local societies have published separate volumes of strays. These are listed in *Current publications by member societies of the Federation of Family History Societies* published by the Federation. The Federation has itself published on microfiche several series of strays collected by the National Strays Coordinator and has distributed copies to local Family History Societies.

The late Mr. H.N. Peyton compiled three typescript volumes of *An index of stray registrations* (1957, 1959, 1962), mainly marriages, at the Society of Genealogists. Also at the Society of Genealogists is a card index, called Index of Migrations, mainly relating to persons going to the Commonwealth and the United States in the nineteenth and twentieth centuries and containing much Canadian material, taken from obituaries in overseas newspapers.

Q. LOCAL INFLUENCES

If failing all the above you are still reduced to drawing a circle on a map with a circumference of ten or fifteen miles and hoping that you will live long enough to shade in all those parishes which will need to be searched for the migrant's baptism you should long ago have considered the geography of the place.

You should look at the one-inch to the mile Ordnance Survey map of the area, not at a simple map showing parish boundaries. See how the parish lies in relation to its neighbours. Look at the direction of the main roads, at the rivers and any unpopulated moor or higher ground. If there is a river or canal consider whether your ancestors were working on it and may have moved along it or perhaps were divided from other places by it. Those on the coast may well be involved in coastal trade and have links in other coastal places.

Look at the direction of the market town and the places regularly visited on that route. Similarly look at the direction of the county town, the whereabouts of the workhouse, the chief parish of the deanery and the hundred. Consider the movement of local officials and of others for trade.

Remember that people did not live in isolation from their contemporaries in the community. They were subject to the same influences. Thus the movement of one documented family may be an indication of the movements of another not so well recorded.

Extended family circles often existed across wide areas of the country and young people in search of work, even when not sure of a place, would at least be sure of bed and board in the household of a distant relative. Families of the same surname in the immediate area of appearance of a migrant who followed the same trade should thus always be investigated. Remember also the circulatory aspect of much migration when people return to the neighbourhood of places with which they are familiar.

Any general history of the area giving details of its economic history and local population movements may thus be invaluable. Of course if your ancestor was a servant in the rectory you will not need indications of this kind, but you will follow the previous movements of the rector. The same applies to any other type of domestic servant or labourer known to be working for a landowner with property in various places. The disposition of that property will need to be considered as well as possible other movements of the master, to fashionable spa towns, for instance, or to London, particularly when a marriage is being sought.

Consider whether the trade followed by your migrant ancestor needed something which only certain areas could give, as Arthur Willis did when tracing his ancestors who were clay tobacco pipe makers in Hampshire (see his *Genealogy for beginners,* London, 1955).

The Census of 1851 for the parish in question, though perhaps much later than your problem, will give a very good idea of the places in the area from which people came and it may be worthwhile to chart out the various places of birth shown in the returns on a map of the area.

Unfortunately there is no recent general bibliography of available local histories. The older ones will be found listed in *The book of British topography: a classified catalogue of the topographical works in the library of the British Museum,* by J.P. Anderson (London, 1881, reprinted 1970) and *A bibliography of British municipal history,* by C. Gross (London, 1915).

The movement of working men generally is considered in *Labour migration in England 1800-1850,* by A. Redford (1926). For the earlier period see P. Clark and D. Souden, *Migration and society in early modern England* (London, 1987).

R. PROVING THE CONNECTION

Once the possible baptism of an ancestor has been found, as much as possible must be done to prove that it is not the correct one, as is done to prove that it is.

In the first place it is essential to see that the baptised child was not buried as a child, did not marry in the immediate area, and did not die there.

The family circle of the child baptised must then be developed, his brothers' and sisters' baptisms and marriages and subsequent histories, and the subsequent history of the parents. Their wills or administrations, and those of uncles and maiden aunts, may need to be searched for (and their deaths if after 1837) in the hope that the migrant may be mentioned. The migrant may be a witness to the marriage of a brother or sister, or perhaps an informant at their deaths.

If the migrant moved at a later stage in his life then some explanation for his disappearance, particularly from taxation records, may be given. The tax collector may explain his inability to collect rates, for instance, by the notation 'gone' or 'run away' in the margin or interleaving of his book. Similar notations may be found in any regular series of payments that may be relevant, e.g. ship money, land tax, or tithe.

If the migrant still had rights to property in the place he left this may appear from the manorial records, and if he held land the Poll Book may show where it was and show his new place of residence elsewhere.

If the migrant left some small congregation of a nonconformist group the records may indicate when he left and to which place he went.

Unfortunately the records of movement out of places are probably less frequent than those into places, and so the proof of connection has to be sought in the development of the family group. Frequently as much weight has to be given to negative considerations as to positive ones.

There are always a few persons who were not migrants but who appear to be newcomers in a particular place because the searches made in earlier records have not been sufficiently wide, because possible variations in surnames have not been taken into account, because nonconformity has not been considered, or even because adoption or the possibility of a change of name has not been entertained. Do not forget to keep an open mind which may admit any possibility.

S. ADDRESSES OF INSTITUTIONS MENTIONED IN THE TEXT

Borthwick Institute of Historical Research, University of York, St Anthony's Hall, Peaseholme Green, York YO1 2PW.

College of Arms, Queen Victoria Street, London EC4V 4BT.

Corporation of London Records Office, P.O. Box 270, Guildhall, London EC2P 2EJ.

Guildhall Library, Aldermanbury, London EC2P 2EJ.

Institute of Heraldic and Genealogical Studies, Northgate, Canterbury, Kent CT1 1BA.

Lambeth Palace Library, London SE1 7JU.

Principal [Probate] Registry of the Family Division, Somerset House, Strand, London WC2R 1LP.

Public Record Office, Ruskin Avenue, Kew, Richmond, Surrey TW9 4DU.

Public Record Office, Chancery Lane, London WC2A 1LR.

Society of Genealogists, 14 Charterhouse Buildings, Goswell Road, London EC1M 7BA.

INDEX

Aberdeen University C.1.
absent voters lists I.4.
Acts, local and personal A.10.
Admiralty officials F.3.
Admiralty, Court of G.2.
adoption M.3.
advertisements C.8.
alehouses *see* publicans
aliases M.3.
almanacs F.3.
Ancestral file O.4.
Angliae notitia F.3.
Annual register B.6.
apothecaries C.5, G.3.
apprentices C.2, K.3.
Arches, Court of A.10, J.2.
architects G.5.
army H.1.
Army List H.1.
artists G.5.
Assize courts J.3.
asylums K.4.
attorneys G.2.

badgers D.3.
bakehouses D.4.
Bank of England B.4.
banns A.7, A.9.
baptisms A.3, B.1.
Baptists A.7, L.1.
barber surgeons C.5, G.3.
barges D.5.
barristers G.2.
Bedfordshire
    apprentices K.4.
    marriages A.4.
beer shops *see* publicans
bell founders G.5.
Berkshire marriages A.4.
Bernau Index J.1.
biographical dictionaries G.5.
Board of Trade officials F.3.
Boards of Guardians K.4.

bookbinders G.5.
boroughs I.2.
Boyd's Marriage Index A.4.
bricklayers C.5.
British imperial calendar F.3.
British Lying-In Hospital K.5.
British Rail F.8.
brokers D.10.
Buckinghamshire apprentices K.4.
burials B.3.

Cambridge University C.1.
Cambridgeshire
    marriages A.4.
    schoolmasters E.1.
canals D.5, F.8, G.6.
canon lawyers G.2.
Canterbury
    freemen C.3.
    marriage licences A.7.
    licences E.1.
    see also Prerogative Court
Catholics A.5, F.2, L.4, L.5.
census returns A.1, B.2, Q.
Chamberlain's Court, London C.5.
Chancery Court J.1.
changes of name M.4.
chaplains G.1.
charity schools C.1.
Cheshire mills K.3, K.4.
Chester freemen C.3.
chief constables F.1, F.6.
chimney sweeps D.12.
Chivalry, Court of J.3, N.
Christian names M.1.
circulating libraries C.8.
Civil Service F.3.
cleaners, railway F.8.
clergy G.1.
clerks, railway F.8.
clock makers G.5.
coastguards G.6, H.4.
coats of arms N.

goldsmiths C.5.
government employees F.3.
grammar schools C.1.
grantees of arms N.
Grays Inn G.2.
Great Yarmouth freemen C.3.
Grocers' Company G.3.
Guildford freemen C.3.
gun licences D.9.
gunsmiths C.5, G.5, G.6.

harbour navigation companies F.8.
hawkers C.5, D.3.
Heralds College
    see College of Arms
Herefordshire marriages A.4.
Hertfordshire
    marriages A.5.
    Quarter Sessions D.
higglers D.3.
high constables F.1, F.6.
Home Office officials F.3.
horners C.5.
hospitals K.4, K.5.
houses of correction K.2.

illegitimacy M.3.
Independents L.1.
Index ecclesiasticus G.1.
Inner Temple G.2.
innkeepers *see* publicans
Inns of Court G.2.
inns *see* publicans
institutions of clergy G.1.
insurance brokers D.10.
interests O.4.
International Genealogical Index
    baptisms A.3.
    marriages A.6.
Isle of Wight marriages A.4, A.5.

Jews A.7, F.2, L.5.
judges G.2.
jurors' lists I.5.

Kent
    marriages A.5.
    newspapers B.6.
kidders D.3.
Kings Bench, Court of K.1.
Kings Lynn freemen C.3.

labourers C.5.
lacemakers G.6.
Lancashire mills K.3, K.4.
Lancaster freemen C.3.
land I.1.
Law List G.2.
lawyers G.2, G.6.
Legacy Duty Office B.4.
Leicester freemen C.3.
letter carriers F.7.
licensed premises D.1, D.2.
lightermen C.5, G.6.
Lincoln's Inn G.2.
Lloyd's captains' register H.3.
local government F.
local histories Q.
London
    burials B.3.
    clergy G.1.
    criminals J.4.
    directories C.7.
    doctors E.1.
    freemen C.5.
    Livery Companies C.5.
    magazine B.6.
    marriages A.4, A.5, A.8.
    nonconformists L.1, L.2.
    parish clerks C.5.
    paupers K.2.
    police F.6.
    wills B.4.
Lord Chamberlain's Department F.4.
Lord Steward's Department F.4.
lunatic asylums K.4.
lying-in hospitals K.5.

Magnae Britanniae notitia F.3.
Manchester Hospital K.5.

poor K.1-4.
porters C.5, F.3.
Post Office workers F.7.
Prerogative Courts of
Canterbury and York B.4.
Presbyterians A.7, L.1.
Principal Probate Registry B.4.
printers C.6, D.6, G.5.
prisoners J.4.
Privy Council,
Judicial Committee A.10.
proctors G.6.
public funds B.4.
public schools C.1.
publicans C.8, D.1.

Quakers A.7, L.3.
Quarter Sessions D.1-11, J.3, K.1.

railwaymen F.8.
Recusant Rolls L.4.
redemption, freemen by C.3.
registers of electors I.4.
religion L.1-6.
removals K.1, K.2.
Residence, Certificates of I.6.
river boatmen G.6.
rogues K.2.
Roman Catholics *see* Catholics
Royal Archives F.4.
Royal College of Physicians G.3.
Royal College of Surgeons G.3.
Royal Commissions
of Inquiry officials F.3.
Royal Household F.4.
Royal kalendar F.3.
Royal Military Academies H.1.
Royal Navy surgeons C.5.

Sacrament Certificates F.2.
sailors *see* seamen
Sandhurst H.1.
schoolmasters E.1.
schools C.1.
sculptors G.5.

seamen H.2, H.3.
poor wives K.5.
searchers of customs F.5.
Secretaries of State officials F.3.
servants Q.
servitude, freemen by C.3.
Settlement Certificates K.1.
sextons E.1.
Sheffield cutlers C.4.
ship brokers D.10.
Ships Musters H.2.
shoemakers G.6.
shopkeepers C.5, D.4.
Shropshire marriages A.4.
silk millers K.3.
silversmiths G.5.
slaughter houses D.4.
Society of Apothecaries G.3.
Society of Friends L.3.
soldiers H.1.
poor wives K.5.
solicitors G.2.
Southwark parish clerks C.5.
St Andrews University C.1.
Staffordshire marriages A.4, A.5.
stationers C.5.
steamship companies F.8.
stockbrokers D.10.
strays P.
Subscription Books E.
Suffolk
apprentices K.4.
marriages A.4.
sugar brokers D.10.
surgeons E.1, G.3.
Royal Navy C.5.
surnames M.2.
sweeps D.12.

tacklehouse and ticket
porters C.5.
taxes R.
tea brokers D.10.
telegraphists F.7.
tilers C.5.